Gregory Campbell
DR. FATHERHOOD

Overcoming A Missing Father

Gregory Campbell

INFINITY PUBLISHING

ISBN 978-1-4958-0512-7
Library of Congress Control Number: 2017915016

Published March 2018

INFINITY PUBLISHING
1094 New DeHaven Street, Suite 100
West Conshohocken, PA 19428-2713
Toll-free (877) BUY BOOK
Local Phone (610) 941-9999
Fax (610) 941-9959
Info@buybooksontheweb.com
www.buybooksontheweb.com

In the Bible, the word father is mentioned more than 1,100 times. The role and presence of a father in the home is significant for the positive mental health development and overall well-being of a child. This book is a must read for men who are dads or aspire to be one someday and for women who were little girls who suffered the absence of their own father......

DR. GERALDINE HICKERSON, DSW, MSW, LCSW

"Too many times I have seen the psychological trauma a missing father can inflict on an individual. I strongly recommend you add this book to your toolkit. "Overcoming a Missing Father" will help you on your journey towards healing.

DR. BRYAN SHAW, Psychiatrist"

"This is a MUST READ" book. The writer is very bold and transparent in sharing personal experiences which are heartfelt and is the great basis for His compassion for Fatherhood. The exercises after each section are thought provoking and soul searching which will surely help all to overcome any strongholds confronted. Most of all you will learn how loving, caring and forgiveness will help you to move on with your life and the God given purpose that has been destined for your success.

JACQUIE DEVEAUX, CSW

Mr. Campbell's "Overcoming a Missing Father" addresses a critical issue in modern culture that is at the root of many of society's most pressing ills. This root is fatherlessness. What makes Mr. Campbell's book so compelling and a must-read is that he doesn't just focus on the problem alone, but instead using lessons learned, provides a practical roadmap for how individuals can overcome the barriers of fatherlessness to thrive and live a life of positive social change.

DR. WILLIAM L. QUISENBERRY,
**Assistant Professor of Organizational Leadership
The Chicago School of Professional Psychology**

CONTENTS

DEDICATION 7
ACKNOWLEDGEMENTS..9
PURPOSE 11
INTRODUCTION..15
WHO SHOULD READ THIS BOOK?...................................19
PERSPECTIVE...33

SECTION I: FATHERLESS VIRUSES............................39

    Fatherless Virus 1: Abandoned 44
    Fatherless Virus 2: Deceased................................49
    Fatherless Virus 3: Incarcerated 52
    Fatherless Virus 4: Drugs or Alcohol 56
    Fatherless Virus 5: Divorced...............................59
    Fatherless Virus 6: Medical Condition 62
    Fatherless Virus 7: Absentee Father
    (*i.e. home, but not involved*) 64
    Fatherless Virus 8: Father's Father.....................67
    Fatherless Virus 9: Military Separation.............69

SESSION II: STRUCTURE 73

    Breaking the Blame Game....................................74
    Abused 81
    Mirror Image...87
    Reflections of Right or Wrong 89
    Breaking the Cycle..93

Borrowed Survival Skills 97
Greg's Circle of Role Models................................ 98
Stepfathers...103
The Flip Side...106

SESSION III: MOVING FORWARD 109

Moving Forward..110
Fresh Start...115
Esteem Yourself..117
Putting the Past Behind 120
Hope...127

DEDICATED TO:

My father, *Roosevelt Campbell Sr.*, for the most part, was a heavy drinker during my childhood. However, dad was simply *a good man* who allowed drinking to take him away from his family responsibilities. He never demonstrated an evil side, like many alcoholics who resorted to beating their wives or children and for that I am truly grateful! Dad taught me to recognize those things to avoid as a father; and though painful, my children have greatly benefited from such lessons. Perhaps, dad was dealing with an undiagnosed case of Post Traumatic Symptom Disorder (PTSD) from his time spent in *Vietnam*. Unfortunately, about the age of 36 he went into an alcohol induced diabetic coma for a period of days. Upon recovery, he remained in the care of his mother for many years and the Veterans Administration (VA) for a couple years prior to his death at age 58. My younger brother, Roosevelt II and I would visit him in Chicago most summers just to help him to remember our names. Years later after joining the army and getting married, my wife, older daughters and I took a few trips to spend time with dad and grandmother. Our final visit was at the Veterans hospital with our younger daughter. Sadly enough, he had gone blind due to diabetes complications, so he was only able to hold, but never saw her. Many years prior to his death in 1995, I decided to love and forgive him no matter what I missed as a child.

Roosevelt Campbell Sr.
(Greg's Father)

Greg (4), Dad &
Roosevelt II (*brother*) (3)
Photos donated by: Family

Dad took these pictures with a million-dollar smile and my choice has been to remember him from these images. Other photos of him simply reflect his wrong choices, inward pain, his Vietnam experiences or potentially a bad marital relationship.

ACKNOWLEDGEMENTS

Most heartfelt gratitude goes out to my late grandparents and foundation makers, **Sellie S.** (*Big Daddy*) **& Gertie Mae** (*Big Mama*) **Smith**. These are my mother's parents and I can say they sacrificed themselves to enrich my personal ventures. They raise their 5 children and the majority of their grandchildren in a very small house. They both were very instrumental in raising and teaching me genuine love, character & responsibility. Big Daddy also taught me how to respect and value money.

"MAMA NEM!!!"

Sellie S. (*Big Daddy*) & Gertie Mae (*Big Mama*) Smith

True Patriarchs

[Photo donated by the family.]

Together Until the End!
[Second photo by: Darwin L. Campbell]
(*Greg's oldest brother*)

Here is a man who worked very hard and made great investments with the knowledge he possessed. My grandmother, like many women, held down the everyday issues by taking care of the home and multiple children. I have great respect for them both as I know it was a challenge and think that many people today avoid their own responsibilities. Even after leaving to join the Army and having a family of my own, going home to visit *"Mama Nem"* was a priority! They are truly missed by everyone they raised, touched and mentored!

"Let's just say, I was raised in the village of responsibility and accountability!"

PURPOSE

The increased absence of biological fathers from homes has been discussed for many years, but the problems associated with fatherlessness continues to grow. My goal and mission is to give purpose and foster hope to the very people negatively impacted from the fatherless plague.

My desire is to share how I overcame those hurtful times and pressed forward in life toward success. The death of a father at a young age can be just as traumatizing as one who leaves to never be seen again. There is no one in the world that hasn't experienced or knows someone who can directly relate to what you are about to read. Personally, I am concerned about discussions not focusing on the root of the catastrophic *Fatherless Viruses* that continues to sweep across the world. We cannot keep putting a bandage on an infected wound and expect it to get better. I do believe there is a cure! Helping you overcome your missing father situation will benefit your family and generations to come.

POINT: *"The Fatherless Viruses or the lack of fathers is not an age, race, nationality or economic status issue. It reaches us all and no one can deny that fact!"*

While many people would have preferred to get straight to the punch and just learn how to get over the absent father, I tend to think there is a grave need to gather reasons first. I will begin by filling this book with enough vital information to help open your eyes to a new way of thinking.

Society is made up of an enormous number of fatherless homes. Those who have both parents are considered to be in a minority situation and that number is only decreasing every year. Each one of us has a role to play in helping change the way people view responsibility as parents. Unfortunately, many parents blame the government and school for their lack of attention to what is clearly their job. Starting with the children at younger ages is very critical, because as a teenager most tend to have become independent thinkers. Raising children to be great productive citizens and parents has taken a backseat far too long, for many parents. One goal for this book is to create a new way of doing what is right. If we take action at the root of the problem, there is a greater chance to see the fruit within! The days where family consist of a man and woman working together to raise their children, must return. The troubled and bitter public in this nation reflects fatherless situations and it is time to help those affected.

"If we take action at the <u>root</u> of the problem, there is a greater chance to see the <u>fruit</u> within!"

Most of us are sent into adulthood like a missile that was not properly programmed to reach its desired destination. There must be a level of wisdom, knowledge and understanding around everyone at a young age in order for them to become effective parents themselves. With that said, fathers are very vital to the complete accomplishment of such attributes. When the head of the family is removed, there is a high percentage chance our youth will continue to miss their mark of success as parents and in many other areas of life. Men and women sometimes grow apart from one another, but the children should not suffer due to their parent's selfish reasons.

For those of you who didn't have a father around and were negatively affected, this book has your name written in it in some form or fashion!

INTRODUCTION

Single mothers or grandparents often fill the gap of irresponsible fathers who are priority challenged. *Wouldn't it be nice to live in a world where both parents were responsible for their children during the growing phase?* This alone would reduce rates of crime, prison crowding, divorce, suicide, hopelessness, a bitter society and much more. Unfortunately, this is a dream and our society has a long way to go to achieve such a goal.

Perhaps your father left before or right after you were born. Maybe divorce or death took him away. Or, maybe he was only around from a physical standpoint. Regardless of which category he fell into, there is always a great deal of pain left for children/adults to endure. This book could have been written about responsibilities or voids of fathers and mothers, but our greater problems in society centers around fathers being absent. With that in mind, my focus will be concentrated on our fathers.

Take a journey with me as I share some of my own unpleasant experiences as a child and young man. These personal experiences will allow me to illustrate various points being made. Arguing, fights, drinking, drugs and finally divorce caused me to rebel and get involved in mischievous activities into my teenage years and adulthood. My personal journey was a worthwhile challenge and as unpleasant as it was I would not change a thing. Now it is time for me to help others prepare for their breakthrough into success and happiness as parents and grandparents. __*In this book*__, you will find various techniques I used to resolve my issues from anger, resentment and even hatred. Additional methods have been included to offer greater opportunities for overcoming pain. To accomplish the healing process, you must first be willing to be open to regaining hidden or suppressed feelings. *Secondly*, you must strive to work on turning bad situations into good ones. I like to refer to that as *"turning lemons into lemonade"*. Before you can erase traumatic events, you must first determine the root cause of the matter. Throughout the contents of this book you will be confronted with many personal questions. Allow them to build foundational thoughts needed to help get you past the hurt, anger and confusion.

There are numerous reasons people are left without a father and the pain and anger left behind can last a lifetime. The majority of people never come to grips with the separation or void. Such understanding and closure can only come when an individual decides to forgive, forget and simply move on into greater potential. Before anyone can begin the process of overcoming not having a father around, they must acquire broad knowledge. What I mean is; when they gain knowledge of the larger picture (*i.e. other types of cases*) understanding will follow. Overcoming such an experience requires a great deal of healing, psychologically and emotionally. You will not find statistics in this book, because the stats that matters most is yours.

Most of us have heard about deadbeat dads and those harsh comments toward them. The list of irresponsible fathers gets larger each year and unfortunately so does the number of affected children. This dilemma will only continue to get worst if people don't harness the root cause. Millions impacted have never gotten beyond anger, hate, disappointment or other life blockers. My goal is to make available pieces of the closure puzzle to launch you forward into a dimension of hope for you and future generations. Please allow me to use my personal experiences to make much of the case for points being made in this book. Thanks, in advance for your understanding!

WHO SHOULD READ THIS BOOK?

Please gain an open mind before reading further, because you are about to cross into the land of reality. Venturing beyond this point will require you to be totally honest with yourselves and address suppressed issues. You will travel back into your subconscious to access various issues of your fatherless childhood and in some cases your adulthood.

**Men** and _**Women**_ of all ages, will certainly benefit from the contents of this book. Everyone either has lived without a father around or know someone presently experiencing the pain associated with such a void. Just maybe the very essence of having this book will assist with bringing millions across the threshold into hope needed to correct negativity plaguing the world.

Anyone who is/was negatively impacted by their biological father not spending quality time with them or have lost him at no fault of his own may benefit from this book. You may find your experience to fit one or more of the following missing major components. Which one(s) apply to you?

CHECK ALL THAT APPLY TO YOUR EXPERIENCES:

_____Have not been told you're beautiful by your father (*Women/Young Ladies*)?

_____Never had a father to teach you how to treat a lady (*Men/Young Men*)?

_____Didn't have a father present to teach by example of the type of man suitable for marriage or father material (*Women/Young Ladies*)?

_____Your father never or rarely attended sport activities you were participating in?

_____Your father doesn't/didn't assist with educational requirements (*i.e. homework, etc.*)?

_____Never was told you are/were _loved_ by your father?

_____Have family members and/or friends whose fathers are or were not involved in their lives?

_____Desire to have a father to share your success stories?

_____Were deprived of being taught life skills (*i.e. how to tie a tie, financial, sports, how to drive, etc.*)?

_____Continuously experience feelings of anger in many situations?

_____Father was taken from you at no fault of his own (*i.e. death, medical, etc.*)?

_____Have behavioral problems that cause you to become aggressive towards authority?

WRITING YOUR OWN, IF NOT COVERED:

_____

_____

IF YOU HAVE CHECKED ONE OR MORE OF THE ABOVE, THIS BOOK IS FOR YOU!!!

<u>NOTE:</u> *You may find there are several listed above which pertains to a friend or family member, so if this book helps you, get them a copy as a gift. You owe it to yourself and others around you to heal. Become an encourager for those who seem to have always struggled with what you are reading in this book.*

"THE <u>HARM</u> OF A MISSING FATHER HAS BEEN DONE, BUT IT'S DAMAGE <u>HAS</u> <u>NOT</u> <u>WON!</u>"

The negative affect of an absent father has no boundaries when age, race, gender or financial status is concerned. Hopefully, realizing who and how broad others victimized by the fatherless issues are, will better your chances of overcoming and helping others do the same. *It was very important to allow readers to experience everyone's situation in order to become stronger and effective in future endeavors.* Complete the entire books contents and you will understand why it includes everyone.

<u>*Please take a moment to read each category below of people this book is meant to assist:</u>

1. Are you a **_YOUNG MAN_** left to learn from the streets about becoming a real man and father?

    You might be a young man whose father never was around to demonstrate character; by saying he loves you or simply by teaching life skills. Due to his not being around, you might have become disruptive at school and refused to obey authority. As I think back to my younger years *"Acting Out"* is what I would call my negative behavior. The very thought of him not being around or seeing others with their fathers tore me up inside, causing me to react and submit to activities that were just wrong!

    Most young men without fathers tend to make bad moves thinking it is correct, yet some of them wise up and make changes early. You must realize all of these things are ingredients for what type of father, person or citizen you will become. The problem is, if you choose to harbor the bad only, you may have children of your own who may need this book as bad or worse than you will. We will further discuss deeper into various situations and options to help take you to another level of thinking, so please just keep reading.

    Your future successes depended on your ability to identify those things that can railroad your growth. Choose to do as I did and change the vicious cycle. Doing what is right puts you into a category of *real men* and nothing else, no matter what the "haters" may call it. I was called every name possible by those men wanting me to follow them into the ditches of failure. Your future generations are dependent upon your choices made today. Don't think you are guaranteed to get it together later, because I want to assure you that is what many fathers think, but sometimes it is too late.

No matter what you have been told, there is a great leader inside of you and it is waiting to come out. So, *STOP* allowing people without character to motivate you into making bad choices that will hinder success in your future.

Don't begin having children only to leave them wondering where their father has gone. Taking responsibility is what can ensure your older years will not be filled with regret and a need to return for help from the children you abandoned.

2. Are you a **<u>YOUNG LADY</u>** who needs to gain knowledge of choosing the right future husband and father of your children?

    Perhaps you are the young lady who didn't have your father or saw him treat your mother with no love and disrespect. Now you are confused as to what type of man to settle for now that it is your turn to be the queen. In most cases, you may have made bad choices based on bits and pieces of information picked up from your surroundings as a child, through movies, music and other misguided friends. You could potentially be on your way toward a lifetime of heartache associated with failed relationships. Find out how to determine ways to pick a winner and get the gold which last forever instead of a piece of wood that will rot every time. I guess the best way to say it is; don't settle for someone like your father if he wasn't true to the cause. The choices you make today will surely impact the future of your children. There are many cases when death caused a father to leave us, but you will find our pain goes deep in the same way, causing us to behave differently. Here are a few questions to think about, so be honest with yourself:

WHAT'S MISSING?

- Do you really know who has the best interest for you?

  - Do you happen to know that most young men say sweet little nothings to girls, get them pregnant and toss them to the side to take care of their child alone?

  - Do you find yourself looking for love in all the wrong places, only to find he has no heart or character? The *hunk* sometimes turns out to be like a *hunk of junk*!

  - Do you sometimes wish your father was there to discuss issues that matter to you?

If you have answered yes to either question, please read further to gain the wisdom and knowledge your missing father failed or was not able to provide you. *STOP* allowing others to dictate how beautiful you are or even your worth. This also includes family and so-called friends. Real friends will focus on helping you improve, so if those around you aren't doing that for you find new friends who will. God has made no mess ups, so you are beautiful and that's that, *PERIOD*!

SPEAK THIS TRUTH OF EXCELLENCE OVER YOURSELF DAILY

*"14 Thank you for making me so **wonderfully** complex! Your workmanship is marvelous – how well I know it."* *Psalm 149:14 NLT*

SPECIAL NOTES:

- *Stop waiting for some guy to speak sweet little nothings, just to give you nothing.*

- *You are beautiful and are not to be anyone's baby factory, so don't be taken by the lies.*

- *Any good man will never cause **physical** or **verbal harm** to you or others. Just don't have a baby by that guy, let him grow up and someone else can have him later!*

- *"Young Ladies, I want you to know that you are beautiful, smart and great things belong to you. Now begin believing it for yourself and stop waiting for anyone else to tell you that. Begin to **Esteem Yourself**!"*

- *What you think about you matter more than anyone else!*

3. Are you a **_MAN_** who never got over your father not mentoring you into manhood or physically

being around? When speaking with numerous of men I realized they have the hardest time dealing with an absent father and end up causing greater pain on others. Maybe you are following the same mold as your own father or worst.

Perhaps you are a man who has lived many years struggling to overcome not having your father present during those important young years of life? Could it possibly be you have allowed the void of your father to hinder your ability to reach your full potential as a real man and father? Many men don't want to expose their weaknesses, because it can tend to show how much they don't know. That thought alone is what has hurt many great men and those they love. Just think, men are supposed to be the head and foundation, but often submit to the lower end of responsibility. The bitterness and hurt from not having a father around can create lifelong scars that foster in bad relationship choices. Many men live their entire life wondering what causes them to repeat the same actions of their fathers. Like most men, my life fell into this category and it lasted well into my twenties. All I knew was that I did not want my own children to remember me as an alcoholic who never provided them with love and support. Like a broken record that played over and over in my mind as I tried to be a husband, father and daily drinker.

Sometimes we harbor the negative of not having our own fathers and frequently affect others around us. When this happens, our children may become rebellious and often seek attention outside of the home (*i.e. school, the streets/gangs, drinking, drugs, sex, etc.*). This is true for our sons and daughters, so the buck must stop with men who desire to be true leaders and not followers of the failing group.

Excuses often lead to regret and none of us really want to look back and say "*I wish I would have, could have.*" As a father, not being involved can result in missing out on what can never be regained, but there is hope for moving forward. Realizing it isn't too late is critical.

There are those who didn't have a father around and just repeated or listened to lies on the streets of what it means to be a man.

REAL MEN

- Do not allow the void of their father be an excuse to *not* after to do what's right!

- Never *abuse* women for any reason!

- Never depend on their *children's mother* or *their grandparents* to take care of their children!

- Never allow *hatred towards or from a child's mother* keep them from their fatherhood duties!

- Are there to change their children's **Diapers** and if not, don't expect those same children to change their **Depends** in old age!

- Take care of every one of their children, no matter how many baby mamas there are!

- Understand, it takes a man to raise a boy to become a man and a father must be a role model for young ladies!

- Lastly, _real_ _men_ are responsible fathers who learn on the job very often!

Most importantly, stop settling for the ignorance of society where you are constantly bombarded with statements that do not provide wisdom toward a greater future. Your purpose in life is to become wise and pass it on to the next generation, not create more babies and not take care of them. Too often we agree with bad advise of others and when we are older realize they made no good sense.

FINALLY: _What will your fatherhood resume say about you when you die? Just something to think about as you may be striving to overcome the void in your own life._

> "REAL
>   MEN
>   ARE
>   RESPONSIBLE
>   FATHERS!"
> _GREGORY CAMPBELL_
> _(Dr. Fatherhood)_

"There's no secret that many Fathers in America have abdicated their roles. All the statistics we see point to a Fatherhood Exodus that is wrecking our society. Despite this, there is reason for hope! Many Fathers are embracing their position as the spiritual leader of their families, and our country and world is better off for it! Statistically and Biblically speaking, *there is no replacement for an engaged Father in the lives of his children."*

MR. KENT EVANS,
Executive Director, Manhood Journey

4. Are you a **WOMAN** (*single or married*) who wants to gain understanding of why some men refuse to step up to the plate of responsibility?

   Many women are victims of having to be a mother and father. The thought of a woman being left alone by fathers to teach sons and daughters what a man should is totally insane. Most single mothers give me a second glance when I say: "It takes a man to raise a boy to become a man and a father must be a role model for young ladies". They are correct to want credit for their efforts and rightfully so. By no means am I attempting to discount the hard work associated with raising children alone. My point is, men are supposed to be the main support beam for raising boys to become responsible and respectful men and act as an example for daughters to pick a caring future husband.

   What I believe this book will offer you:

   - *Understand how losing your father in any manner affects your everyday relationships.*

   - *How to get beyond the lack of a father figure.*

- *Observe ways to determine which negative experiences are working against you and your success.*

- *How to harness the greatness inside of you.*

- *Gain greater understanding on how having a relationship with someone else who lacked a father may affect your future.*

- *A sense of purpose and to show you how important you really always have been.*

- *Do you find yourself looking for love in all the wrong places, only to find he has no heart or character? The* **hunk** *sometimes turns out to be a* **larger pile of junk in your trunk!**

If you can relate to either statement or question, please read further to gain the wisdom and knowledge your missing father failed or was not able to provide you. You are here for a greater purpose and gathering the tools to succeed is critical!

"Ladies, I want you to know that you are beautiful, smart and great things belong to you. Now begin believing it for yourself and stop waiting for anyone else to tell you that. Begin to **Esteem Yourself!***"*

The word father has been broken down to demonstrate how important they are to their children and what is missed when syndromes are involved:

- **F = Friend & Foundation** – Truly a person who cares creates an atmosphere which will develop stability that is solid as a rock.
- **A = Advisor** – Life is like a championship basketball game. A great coach is required to win the game.
- **T = Teacher** – When leading by example help produce tools and methods required to prepare children for future success.
- **H = Humility** – Not allowing self-centered desires to become priority over the little ones who need them most.
- **E = Endurance** – A willingness to stay the course of raising our nations valuable future leaders, no matter what obstacles arise.
- **R = Reliable** – Trustworthy to a point where sacrifice becomes second nature to becoming a man of his word.

We all know there are no substitutes for a father's love or involvement. Various things are used by many men to take the place of their presence. *For example:*

- Money
- Cars
- Pets
- Toys
- Expensive vacations

Those materialistic things are not noticed by a small child and when they are older, they are smart enough to know much more is missing. Many of us have experienced these types of additives and some of us wish those things could have been replaced with developed memories. No matter whether you are male or female the need to address the void is very critical for society to improve.

"I believe this book will be very helpful to young people and adults as they strive for a better, more successful life."
Marion Peeler, MS Counseling & Education (27 years)

PERSPECTIVE

While writing the *"Who Should Read"* section, it became obvious that my audience needed to consist of a broad spectrum. Our present behavior may often be associated with the emotional past experiences we had no control of as children.

Understanding what we experienced as children will assist us in going from victim to victorious. Overcoming requires a strong desire from a person to want to become better or provide more for their children than they received. My idea of overcoming is strongly motivated by a need to help stop the bleeding of hurting hearts that do/didn't have father involvement. Unfortunately, some lose fathers from medical and death reasons, but as I told my children my goal when raising them was to be there and share until I no longer could. I wanted them to be prepared, if something were to happen to me. Through this book, I want to use an unselfish approach and spread my concept! Handling the truth is the most important factor in reaching closure with any unpleasant situation we will encounter.

After speaking with hundreds of people either in prison, jail or those free in society, I've learned that most who lacked a fathers' presence harbored a bitter taste. These people top the number of those who have committed crimes, gotten pregnant at an early age, used drugs, drank alcohol, or many other unthinkable acts. I don't take this lightly and neither should you, because each one of us without fathers fall into one of those virus categories.

Please stay with me, if you are or know someone who fit those indicated in the *"Who Should Read"* section. The contents of this book should help take you beyond the stage of undesirable into a mode of hope. There are many people you personally know who may be able to use these techniques and benefit from them in their future generations.

I will remind you from time to time about the similar pain associated with losing a father due to death. Not all of us lost a father behind a lack of responsibility and it needs to be clear that not having him in any way is hurtful. Your journey and newly gained knowledge may or may not alter your father behavior, but it can surely help you view life differently. What I am sharing with you are life applications designed to take you from this point. Becoming agitated is normal, so I would recommend you continue reading until it goes away. Please do not let unhappy or bitter feelings stop you from at least trying to see what can be improved about your life.

Those of us who have been negatively affected by our fathers will sometimes suppress reality. What I mean is; the pain can be purposely hidden in order for us to maintain a sense of sanity. I can comfortably say pain from my father's limited involvement has been eliminated only after many years of personal healing. As we progress through this book I will continue to make thought provoking statements. Once again, my goal is to ask you questions which will foster turning your ***lemons*** into _lemonade_. Trust me, for me it was a great deal of time before a smile or happiness manifested. Each one of us has a different story and some of the lemons possessed are numerous, but the size of the positive blessing container is up to you.

With strict honesty ask yourself; do you really care about getting beyond hurt and pain brought on from an absent father?

Are you one of the following or more?

1) Tired of constantly having failed relationships? _____

2) Constantly losing jobs? _____

3) Not able to concentrate on the things that matter? _____

4) Always <u>angry</u> or having mood swings? _____

You may just simply be suffering from the **_Without A Father Syndrome (W.F.S.)._** You won't find this in a medical book, but it is fitting for the category of symptoms. If honest, most of us are or were driven to live with one or many listed symptoms in the chart below.

<u>YOUR INITIAL SYMPTOMS</u>

Mark the initial symptom status that relates to your fatherless and personal situation. Please approach them with openness and honesty, because you will need to refer to your selections at the end of the book. **_Without A Father Syndrome (W.F.S.)_** has negatively affected millions in this country and most deal with these symptoms:

TODAYS DATE: _____

FEELINGS & ISSUES	GREG'S EXPLANATIONS	MARK ALL THAT APPLY
Abandoned	Father gone without a trace.	
Abused	Being physical, mental or sexually mistreated.	
Abusive	Tend to physically, verbally or psychologically mistreat those you suppose to love.	
Anger	Bitter feelings on a constant basis toward others.	
Depressed	Lack of an ability to function due to unpleasant situations.	
Dysfunctional	Family social breakdown that hinders proper all-around growth of a child into adulthood.	
Forgotten	Refuse to allow your heart to heal from the pain of rejection.	
Frustration	Living a life where nothing satisfies you.	
Guilt	Feel responsible for your father's departure.	
Hateful	Make everyone around you miserable.	
Hopelessness	View everything (*i.e. relationships, career, yourself, etc.*) as not valuable.	
Hurt	Allow your pain to negatively affect others around you (*i.e. family, friends, co-workers, etc.*)	
Ignored	Viewed as the little duckling that never would or will become anybody special (*i.e. parents, friends, boss, co-workers, etc.*).	
Low self-esteem	Can't think highly of yourself, even when others do.	

Mourning	Have lost a father by death and can't seem to stop allowing grief to get in the way of life matters.	
Rejected	Feel everyone has turned their backs on you.	
Resentment	Harbor bitter feelings that cause you to act inappropriately.	
Sad	Constantly hurting inside for losing your father with very little relief.	
Safety (*Unsafe*)	Never feel or felt protected or valued.	
Shame	Embarrassed of how you look, speak or of your past.	
Shy	Prefer being alone most of the time.	
Tormented	Experiencing continual stress or agitation from within for some odd reason.	
Unloved	Feel no one loves you or never has.	
Unsociable	Hard to communicate with others and build healthy relationships.	
Unstable Relationships	Can't seem to settle down and take life serious.	
Violence	Either gravitates to abusive relationships or is abusive.	
Worthlessness	Think you have to add value in society because of your given situation.	
You may place additional symptoms and your personal definitions below:		

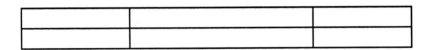

Some may decide my definitions are either too harsh or not aggressive enough. That is totally understandable, so please take the liberty to re-write them according to your desire. *This book and its contents are all about you, so tailor it to yourself.*

This area is just a taste of a roller coaster ride that will be worthwhile upon completion, so please stay focused. We must get through the dark tunnel and remove all distractions before reaching the prize. Trust me, there were times while writing this book when my mind drifted back into a mode of disappointment. There are many reasons for losing our fathers, but I assure you there is a time to stop living in pain and begin living in gain.

NOTE: *We will revisit this later to see how the contents have helped you move beyond this present status or whether more time will be required.*

FATHERLESS VIRUSES

- Fatherless Virus #1: Abandoned
- Fatherless Virus #2: Deceased
- Fatherless Virus #3: Incarcerated
- Fatherless Virus #4: Drugs or Alcohol
- Fatherless Virus #5: Divorce
- Fatherless Virus #6: Medical Condition
- Fatherless Virus #7: Absentee Father
  (*i.e. in the house, but not involved*)
- Fatherless Virus #8: Father's Father
- Fatherless Virus #9: Military Separation

Many of us can easily identify with more than one virus and know that viruses can kill. In most cases, the presence of one generally creates a vacuum for others to exist and tend to kill those very things that matter. For that reason alone, I felt it was necessary to include all eight in this book to allow each reader an opportunity to explore all options. Most of these viruses were early enemies in my life and I will share personal accounts to make my points. Please keep in mind that this book is about you or those you may help and not strictly about myself.

FATHERLESS VIRUSES

My young mind could not conceive what was happening as I witnessed the use of alcohol and constant arguing between my mother and father. There never seemed to be a moment of peace where I'd feel secure while they were married. During most of my younger years similar questions such as; *"Why was dad out of the loop?"* played like a broken record in the back of my mind. Quite often it raised its ugly head as I struggled to identify who I was and how to gain life skills. While preparing to write this book, I found myself reliving those very moments which affected me prior to my healing experience. It is devastating for children to live in conditions where their father doesn't exist, passes away or he is there but, simply ignores those who need him most. We all know the man is supposed to be the leader, provider and most importantly the protector. However, the truth is society has embraced just the opposite in many cases.

Before proceeding, we must understand why a father may have not been available. Society tends to focus on the hurting people affected by what many call a *"deadbeat dad"*, but as you can see the focus has been broadened. There are so many ways to have lost a father and I want to address several other causes, with an understanding that some may not be represented. The purpose is to create dialogue or an avenue that will allow you to realize we all need basic remedies to help us overcome. It is like five people breaking their right leg in five different accidents and all being healed from one standard method. Of course, some legs will heal differently depending on the break and physical condition of the patient. All approaches in this book will not work to overcome every missing father in the same time frame. However, there is one thing for certain, a start toward healing will occur when an open mind is involved.

A critical question to address is: *What causes us to carry anger and not release its vice?* Deep down inside of all of us is an event or a series of events that have negatively affected us. It is easy to say I forgive, but for most the forgetting part is nearly impossible to shake. I have personally found a way to get beyond the hurt and recycle it into opportunities. In the chapter *"Moving Forward"* we will focus on various options to help bring the hurt from within and gain control. Before reaching that point we must cover several important issues from a realistic point of view.

We have constantly heard people mention how bad fathers must be forced to change or be punished. In most cases, many of them end up in either having major misfortunes, prison or in a cemetery; and much is unknown about their own stories. My concern is that not many of us are looking at the root of *why* or *how* fatherless dilemmas occur. We are first looking at the individual and then will attempt to use disciplinary measures to correct their behavior.

Take a minute to review the different reasons I would like to examine *"Fatherless Viruses"* which are tearing down society. The listed viruses seem to be appropriately titled, because they have the potential to negatively affect the body and mind for a lifetime. As you will see, not all of them are by choice!

See which one of the "Fatherless Viruses" have plagued your life?

*(**NOTE:** No need to answer the question(s), because you may do so after the explanations and allow your feelings, emotions, disappointments, anger, etc. to develop).*

1. Were you **_Abandoned_** before birth, at birth or during childhood?

2. Did your father **_Pass Away_** during your childhood?

3. Has your father been **_Incarcerated_** for an extended period?

4. Was **_Drugs or Alcohol_** the cause of his absence?

5. Did you watch your parents go through a bitter **_Divorce_**?

6. Did a **_Medical Condition_** make him unable to physically participate?

7. Was he an **_Absentee Father_** (*i.e. he is in the house, but not involved*)?

8. What if your **_Father's Father_** was not there for him?

9. Did **_Military Separation_** cause separation?

1	2	3	4	5	6	7	8	9

Each one of these mentioned could truly represent the root cause for most fathers not being present when it matters. The questions or reasons provided may seem to be very blunt, but I feel it is very important to be realistic when discussing overcoming a father's absences. If either one of those listed have aggravated or saddened you, just stop and take a deep breath. That reaction is exactly what's expected and is the foundation towards overcoming. Many of these reasons are not discussed in family settings for one reason or another. I must say, this is part of the problem and I want to be the first to begin a national trend to correct this dysfunction. There are many reasons for homes to become unstable, but I will be addressing issues that I feel are of greater need.

"Every circumstance discussed may appear to be different, but the depths of pain remain the same."
Gregory Campbell
(Dr. Fatherhood)

NOTE: Please take a few moments to read each one of the *Fatherless Viruses, even if you didn't experience a particular fatherless situation.* What you read will not only help you, it may just be what a friend or family member needs to know. Now let's explore the various viruses in greater deal:

FATHERLESS VIRUS #1: ABANDONED

It's pathetic for self-centered men to not provide some level of concern for their children. At any rate, this makes me think of only one word "*Abandonment*". There are cases where a father will decide to disappear upon hearing of pregnancy or leave when the going gets rough. I think they mistake the old saying: "*When things get tough the tough gets going*". We all know that means to buckle down and work things out no matter how hard it may become. When responsibility is required many people choose to take the road that hurts others and unfortunately this is somewhat the norm in society today. Many people can understand why fathers are rarely given a shout out from sports figures or the music world. The way I see it, cowards do not deserve to be credited for things they did not do. Some men will refuse to be there when it is **_diaper_** buying and changing time, but will expect the children they abandoned to be there to change their **_depends or diapers_** when they're older. That is plain, simple and true. However, there is that one child who has a big enough heart to take care of a father he or she barely or didn't know.

Would you help your father if he abandoned you and later in life needed your help? Explain why or why not.

_____

_____

_____

_____

_____

Perhaps he was married to another woman and other children were also a part of the equation. This is often the situation that we only find out in adulthood when we search or are asked to attend his funeral. Years ago, when the song "*Papa was a rolling stone*" played on the radio I felt somewhat embarrassed, because I didn't know if my father was one or not. For those of you too young to know what that meant, let me enlighten you on the subject. Many fathers have no concern about staying in one location and raising a family. Some men are insecure when responsibility is involved and think the grass is greener on the other side. Needless to say, the fatherless situations have become the norm for decades in America. In fact, I would venture to say those who have or had fathers at home are considered *the minority*. As I said there will be no statistical data, but to prove my point just ask at least ten people and see for yourself.

Most young men having a child become scared or cowardly and rather than stay to take on their responsibilities they run for cover. Many of us had bad role models and didn't know how to do what was right by our children. Fortunately, this is not the case for everyone. Becoming a father at 18 years old of twin girls had its challenges, but I was determined to do what was right. Over 30 years later I am still around to nurture my grandchildren.

Millions of people are growing or have grown up without the presence of their biological fathers around. Just the thought creates a level of anger in the minds of people not even directly affected. Those impacted by neglect have more than anger to deal with. They're constantly reminded of a father who should be there providing support during Christmas, birthdays, sporting events, graduations, illnesses and much more.

Let's briefly explore some reasons surrounding the abrupt departures that eventually hurt others:

Several root causes for abandonment:

1. *Rejection* by the mother in such a way that it becomes hurtful or shameful for him to stick around. This is one thing generally over-looked when we see men leaving home and not looking back. By no means is this a good excuse, but there are cases where a non-supportive woman will keep even a good man from his children. When a man is rejected, pride and ego kick in and the defensive phase follows. Self-preservation becomes his weakness causing him to make bad choices. Just remember, maybe he was ignored as a child and never got over such an experience or hurt.

   QUESTION: What reasons would you feel someone may have gotten rejected?

   1. _____   4. _____

   2. _____   5. _____

   3. _____   6. _____

2. _Fear_ is one thing that will hinder progress or even an attempt to reach success. The concern of not feeling he can live up to the responsibilities of being a good parent may cause fear. Many younger men feel they will not be good fathers simply because of the lack of knowledge handed down to them. Maybe someone told them they would never or can't do anything right. Most people believe those types of statements.

   QUESTION: _What reasons would you add to show how fear could motivate departure?_

   1. _____   4. _____

   2. _____   5. _____

   3. _____   6. _____

3. _Immaturity_ hinders them from gaining the wisdom and knowledge required to care for another person outside of themselves. Perhaps their parents or a single mother never allowed them to mature into a responsible young man. This issue has always been controversial when I speak with single mothers, but most have agreed once I explain myself. Just think, how can they do right by their own family or children if they have been enabled by parents?

   QUESTION: _What immature behavior came to your mind?_

   1. _____   4. _____

   2. _____   5. _____

   3. _____   6. _____

4. *Selfish reasons* are an issue which remove men from the areas of responsibility before they truly realize how important their involvement is to their children. Being too lazy to keep a job or having another financial obligation can easily create problems.

QUESTION: *Can you think of other self-centered activities, behaviors or excuses that take fathers out of the picture?*

1. _____   4. _____

2. _____   5. _____

3. _____   6. _____

FATHERLESS VIRUS #2: DECEASED

Some fathers die before making a needed contribution in their children's lives. Clearly a case that is uncontrollable, unless the person took his or her life. This loss is an irreversible situation which causes a void not like any other we will discuss. This death may have come through fault or uncontrolled reasons and this category must have a place in this book. A loss by any reason or age always creates a missed opportunity to gain wisdom, having a male role model or receive love from a father with care and character. In either case, you were placed into a fatherless void that may cause you to wonder what could have been.

While at the age of 9 or 10 my father went into an alcohol induced diabetic coma and when he recovered much of his memory of his family was gone. He did eventually relearn who much of the family members were, but that was about it. He required assistance and health care from around the age of 36 until his death at age 58. You might be wondering why I have mentioned my father in this section. In some odd way, I felt he had died at 36, even though he lived for another 20 years. The void of his involvement took its toll on my young mind.

It was July 8, 1995, when my father passed away and a sense of anger still festered within my heart. Even a year or so after the funeral I realized my negative feelings had not been completely resolved. Of course, I had expressed love toward him many years before his death, but the verbal forgiveness never took place between dad and I. His mind never regained enough for me to express my disappointments and create a true father son bond from that point. In his defense, he was no longer physically able to return to his responsibilities, leaving my siblings and I alone to manage emptiness!

Perhaps you had a similar situation or simply lost your father at a young age. As you may already know there are a massive number of people who have similar stories to tell, so you are definitely not alone.

QUESTIONS:

1. *Have you personally experienced the loss of your father? _____ If so, what age were you? _____*

2. *What do you wish your father could have done with you as a child or adult?*

   1. _____   4. _____

   2. _____   5. _____

   3. _____   6. _____

3. *Do you feel this experience caused missed opportunities, failed relationships, etc.? Explain.*

   _____

   _____

   _____

   _____

   _____

   _____

4. *List a few things you are grateful to have learned in his absence (i.e. One of mine is: having learned how to be a responsible husband and father).*

1. _____   4. _____

2. _____   5. _____

3. _____   6. _____

NOTE: *Later we will present a tool which should help you get past the void of losing a father before mends or opportunities could be established.*

FATHERLESS VIRUS #3: INCARCERATED

Outside of abandonment or the death of a father, an extended incarceration could be the next most devastating way to not have a father present in such critical moments. This void becomes much harsher when fathers do not properly communicate with a child over the years as they grow up. While watching a show about people being locked up for extended periods of time it was obvious by comments made that the inmates sincerely missed their children. The saddest part is those children are being hit even harder than they could ever imagine as they are in so many ways serving time themselves. They are incarcerated in a world without the one who should be there to protect, teach and love them. It is odd, but true, that many children experience much of the same type of separation even while their fathers are free. Just look around your own community or watch the news where you will constantly hear or see child abuse or neglect situations. They generally are locked up for drugs, murder, theft and much more, but in every case such behavior could have been avoided. Many of these men are fathers of hurting children needing them there to nurture and love them. However, their own fathers may not have instilled the needed tools.

As years progressed, there are thousands of young men and women following their fathers' footsteps to only end up in prison. In some instances, they are locked up at the same time and in some cases in the same facility. When a father is not around to be a part of his/her life during the bridge from a child to adulthood, they are definitely harmed in some way. During a speaking event at a prison, I asked the nearly 200 men present: *"How many of you didn't have your fathers in your lives?"* Then I asked: *"How many of you are fathers?"* In shock, I looked around to see that practically all of them had raised their hands after each question. Many of them came down and spoke with me afterward and expressed a desire to make the role of fatherhood a priority. My challenge was for them to not make the same mistake their fathers did to them. As I could tell from speaking with them, many were great men who had made bad choices and ended up in prison. The unfortunate fact is the children are suffering and missing the most out of the deal. Some things happen by accident or out of our control, but criminal behavior is truly by choice. The worst part is many people live life like it's a game, by operating within the realm of what many have called the *"revolving door"* effect. My thoughts are that, when many people have been locked up on a continual basis there is either a concern that immaturity, bitterness or lack of concern is in play. Let's be clear, there are many cases where people have been <u>wrongfully accused</u> and have served time. In those cases, children and even grandchildren were punished.

QUESTIONS:

1. *Has your father been incarcerated during your childhood?*
   _____

2. *How many years was he incarcerated during your childhood years?* _____

3. *How many years were during your adult years?*
   _____

4. *How old were you when he was initially incarcerated?*

_____

5. *What do you wish your father would have done with you as a child or adult?*

1. _____

2. _____

3. _____

4. _____

5. _____

6. _____

6. *Briefly explain your experience and how you were negatively impacted during those separated years? (Use additional page, if necessary)*

_____

_____

_____

_____

_____

_____

_____

_____

_____

_____

_____

_____

_____

_____

FATHERLESS VIRUS #4: DRUGS OR ALCOHOL

Alcohol and drug usage can potentially go down in history as being the major reasons for ripping a father from his post of responsibility. Unfortunately, many children are forced to live in an environment where both of these are being used right in front of them. This behavior only creates an atmosphere or climate that leads to make children think it is normal. I experienced watching not only my father drink like there was no tomorrow, but others in my family had the bad habits of drinking. Their actions made many of the children in the family follow suit. When thinking back, I can easily say my childhood was like a prison sentence of hopelessness. I picked up those very habits for many years before stopping the use of alcohol around 1990. Odd to say, that as a child I hated seeing others do those things and eventually still picked them both up for some years. Of course, drinking was my worst enemy. The simple fact was I felt both were alright initially, because of the broad acceptances, perceptions, and constant exposures when I joined the army in 1979.

Maybe you have your own unpleasant experience of drugs or alcohol exposures or personal usage, or there may be family or friends. It has become the norm for many of us to repeat the very things we see our own parents, relatives or friends do and how each individual outcome varies. The financial burden brought on from using these substances are directly related to poverty and low education levels in this country. Yet we tend to still place the blame on Washington and the school systems. This is something worth discussing and if our politicians truly cared about the well-being of citizens they would aggressively address the harm alcohol creates in the life of users.

I understand that this is a touchy subject to address, because it exposes the ones you love no matter what they have done.

QUESTIONS:

1. *Were you exposed to drugs or alcohol at a young age in your home by family or friends of the family?* _____

2. *Which one(s) were you exposed to?* _____

3. *If you used either, which one(s) did you feel it was alright to use since those around you did it so openly?*

_____

_____

_____

_____

_____

_____

_____

_____

_____

4. *How did it make you feel as you experienced such exposure to this behavior?*

_____

_____

_____

5. *Do you want or care that someday your children might use either? _____ Why or why not (explain)?*

_____

_____

_____

_____

_____

_____

FATHERLESS VIRUS #5: DIVORCE

Divorce is one other corrosive situation in a child's early years which may have a lasting negative impact on future behavior. Watching my parents display continuous anger between one another, while they should have been teaching me how to love, surely caused me confusion. In my personal case, the split of my parents seemed to have been my fault. I remember a heated argument took place after my father hit me with a metal rod used as a barbeque grill charcoal poker. After the divorce, I have always retained some guilt, since I clearly remember the events leading up to the separation.

More than often our first line of defense is to say we forgive, but in our hearts, we can't forget and I am no different. There was a level of hatred in my heart for both parents many years after the divorce was final, but as I got older it began to be released. Realizing early in my adult years that hate was harming my potential growth, I decided to make necessary attitude adjustments. Our feelings toward our parents are very critical and must be addressed, if we want to gain and maintain blessings of success. We can easily allow the relationship our parents had to follow us into our own relationships, only to see them when we look in the mirror.

The outcome of many divorces reminds me of times when my grandmother would walk out into the yard, grab a chicken, and cut its head off in preparation for supper. The *head (father)* would become motionless, but the *body (wife & children)* flopped, flew, twisted, jerked and whatever else while all along slowly dying. This is not always the scenario with the family, because many men do step up to the plate in a greater way. I do commend those of us who are responsible, so some might ask why I shared such a gruesome event. This is how families respond to their missing part of the body. When the father is detached and isn't there to lead the family, the foundation crumbles emotionally and spiritually in more cases than not. Separation of the head from the body caused the body to slowly begin the dying process. Eventually, in most cases the financial and discipline issues rise up in a very bad way. As mentioned, there are fathers with character and passion to do what is right by their children no matter what transpired between the father and the mother. I _do not_ want to sound like all divorced fathers are bad men, because many of us know that isn't true. It is also very important to share that children are not always driven to abuse and crime. Some of the most successful people in society have come out of disadvantaged or broken homes.

When both parents are not actively participating in teaching their children life skills the door of failure will more than likely be opened.

QUESTIONS:

1. *At what age were you when your parents divorced?*

   _____

2. *Did you rebel against one or both parents? If yes, which one and why?*

   _____

   _____

   _____

3. What do you wish your father could have done with you as a child or adult?

   1. _____

   2. _____

   3. _____

   4. _____

   5. _____

   6. _____

4. Briefly explain your feelings about their divorce and how you feel you were negatively impacted?

   _____

   _____

   _____

   _____

FATHERLESS VIRUS #6: MEDICAL CONDITION

Severe medical conditions can be the primary reason for a father not to be directly involved in the nurturing of his children. We must take this fact into consideration when accessing a father's position or status. I had mentioned my father's medical condition which eventually took his life, but I saw fit to touch on it again in this section. As mentioned earlier, an alcohol induced coma stole my father's memory around age 36, causing him to not recognize family for some time. He died at age 58 and opportunities for him to correct the negative past ended twenty years earlier. In my case, here was a man who chose to drink his life away and his actions hurt the children.

Of course, there are many medical conditions that leave men unable to take care of themself or anyone else. This is very unfortunate for children who do not have a clue as to what has occurred and a greater level of harm is involved. Many thoughts of wondering why will travel in the minds at an early age and then into adulthood. One in particular sticks with me; *when I see other fathers doing things with their children my mind begins to think, what if my father and I could have had that experience.* Even as we get older the thoughts are still lingering no matter whether we have gained greater knowledge of the situation. The simple fact is, he wasn't there when I needed him as a child and transitioned into manhood.

QUESTIONS:

1. *Were you a child or adult when your father became medically unable to participate in various activities with you?* _____

2. *What age were you when your father became too ill to participate?* _____

3. *What activities do you wish your father could have done with you as a child or adult?*

   1. _____   4. _____

   2. _____   5. _____

   3. _____   6. _____

4. *Briefly explain your feelings or emotional state during those years and now.*

   _____

   _____

   _____

   _____

FATHERLESS VIRUS #7: ABSENTEE FATHER

While attending a conference filled with thousands of men, a speaker mentioned the term *Absentee Father. The basic definition is when a father is home, but does not actively participate in parenting responsibilities!* In many cases, he is living in the home and paying bills, but have very little if any dealings with the children. After receiving an explanation many men around the stadium gave me the appearance that they could relate to what was described. This reminds me of a game played by children called *"Peek-A-Boo".* His personality demonstrates the *"now you see me, now you don't"* concept. These fathers continuously take credit for raising the great and successful kids when they had very little to do with nurturing them. When both parents are not actively involved with teaching their children life skills there is always increased room for failure.

Quite often mothers are solely supporting their children's activities (*i.e. sporting events, school meetings or lunches, plays, birthday parties and even church attendance*). My children had me there for homework, class projects, school lunches, sporting events, marching band, illnesses, preparing their meals and much more. Keep in mind, my wife was also there participating in those activities. Now grown with children of their own I can truly say, they are excellent mothers and my being the involved father contributed to that outcome.

None of this means he didn't love them, but there are reasons for his inability or desire to be more involved.

QUESTIONS:

1. Was your father home, but rarely involved with you as a child? _____

2. Do you feel your life could have been much better with greater involvement from your father? _____

3. What do you wish your father would have done more of with you as a child?

   1. _____   4. _____

   2. _____   5. _____

   3. _____   6. _____

4. How did you feel when you saw other children doing things with their father?

   _____

   _____

   _____

5. As an adult, do you still think much about the void in your father's presence?

   _____ In what way?

   _____

   _____

   _____

   _____

FATHERLESS VIRUS #8: FATHER'S FATHER

The majority of fatherless cases in this country are products of generational lapses in responsibility. Often while speaking with other men I find most stories are the same in regards to their father's father. My father's father was not around when I was a child, so I would assume he wasn't there for Dad. The unknown is what most of us have lived by and have no clue why our fathers seem to not care. This is by no means an excuse to avoid doing what is right by their own children, but it is obvious the void negatively impacted them and their ability to function properly. To the defense of a fatherless father there is a huge chance he had no clue of how to be a father. I only mentioned one generation, but just think of how far the fatherless viruses went back.

QUESTIONS:

1. Did you know your father's father as a child?
   _____

2. If yes, was he responsible or active in your father's life?
   _____

3. Were there similar habits between your father and his father? _____

   If applicable, list those you are aware of:

   1. _____   4. _____

   2. _____   5. _____

   3. _____   6. _____

4. *Do you feel your father's father could have been a big reason your father turned out the way he did?* _____ *Explain your thoughts for the response.*

_____

_____

5. After going through all of the viruses and addressing appropriate questions which applied, do you feel a need to read onward? _____ Why?

_____

_____

FATHERLESS VIRUS #9: MILITARY SEPARATION

Earlier my father was mentioned about his Vietnam tour and there was clearly a part of that which hindered his ability to have a more involved role as a father. There was something going on in his mind that caused his behavior toward the use of alcohol. As I have gotten older and am speaking to soldiers and veterans about their own personal actions, it is obvious my father was self-medicating to hide memory pains inside.

The summer of 2016, while attending a cookout hosted by my neighbor there was a young man there who opened my eyes to an old problem that is occurring now. Military deployments which have caused extensive separation and even the loss of a father's life is something that has happened since the first military operation. My personal concern is there has always been some sort of a war happening. Maybe not with intentional motives, but a large segment of the unaffected society attempts to push those impacted to get over the lost and move on. The problem is, like with the permanent divide, there is no way to completely let go of a pain that might never go away. Unless the child does not remember their father, it is very difficult to live up to the *"Get Over It"* concept. Generally, most people have a heart of gold when it comes to helping others get beyond painful events, but most of us may just simply do not know what or how to speak words to those who have lost a loved one. *Depending on the support base for the children in a lost or extended separation the negative long-term impact can be devastating!*

In my personal case, there were several voids experienced during my father's time deployed during the Vietnam conflict when I was very young. In fact, I can easily say my opinion about war in general has been formed from my experiences. Love over war can be the ingredient to build stronger families and a better society around the world, but many are not looking at the poison of hatred being spread.

QUESTION:

1. Did your father spend time away from you as a child when serving in military combat missions? _____. If so, explain what you remember of his involvement while home during your younger years?

   _____

   _____

2. Did you lose your father during a military conflict? _____

3. Do you feel your life experiences from his absence was hard on your personal growth? _____

   Explain your response, if you can at this point.

   _____

   _____

   _____

   _____

   _____

Separation is never a good thing for a small child. In my case, there have been years of my being able to discuss my feelings of how the Vietnam War negatively affected my life.

In either virus case, the family is left with a void that may cause major instability and structural damage. As you may have noticed or know there are some situations that cannot be controlled. Nevertheless, we are going to focus on all of those mentioned.

There may be more topics worth addressing when it comes to reasons a father wasn't there, but those included should represent the larger number of us affected. We needed to first address these causes before reaching out for solutions that will prove to be universal when overcoming is involved. Searching for a quick fix to such a complex issue will only lead you nowhere very fast. I hope to have provided you with an awareness to get beyond the hurt or anger by the time you have completed the chapter titled "*Moving Forward*".

SESSION II:

STRUCTURE

- **BREAKING THE BLAME GAME**
- **ABUSE**
- **MIRROR IMAGE**
- **REFLECTIONS OF RIGHT OR WRONG**
- **BREAKING THE CYCLE**
- **BORROWED SURVIVAL SKILLS**
- **GREG'S CIRCLE OF ROLE MODELS**
- **STEPFATHERS**
- **THE FLIP SIDE**

BREAKING THE BLAME GAME

Often victims of various acts, to include *"Fatherless Viruses"* find themselves placing blame on everyone except the root of the problem (i.*e. themselves, their own children, spouses, other relationships, etc.*). Watching my parents' marriage dissolve after my father gave me a *rare* whipping for something I had no control over made me feel responsible for their divorce. I felt very bad inside, blamed myself and simply never told anyone until I had reached my adult years. Noticing my parents' dysfunctional behavior towards one another gave me concern for our well-being. On several occasions after experiencing their drinking and fighting, I would run and get under my bed to feel safe. Knowing they did love us gave me comfort to some extent, but being a protective and responsible big brother caused me to err on caution. This experience created more confusion than any child should have to deal with, so feeling my way through was stressful. There was a little voice telling me *"your bad childhood experiences were all your fault"*. I believed those inward lies and my blame game kicked in causing me to make many wrong choices as I branched into my teen years. Anger and disappointment caused me to withdraw from even expressing sadness during my father's funeral or even placing trust in others. My agitation was fueled from the fact that he never had an opportunity to get it right as a father, due to major permanent medical issues. This is what happens when men neglect their responsibility, become incapacitated or die before realizing their children need them. You too may have had or are still experiencing this type of situation and felt trapped.

As I had gotten older, it became obvious that both of my parents had issues and just maybe I wasn't the cause of their divorce after all. When thinking back it was evident their marital train wreck was strictly caused by their own behavior and nothing to do with me. Gradually, freedom from the blame game started breaking away like scales, but deep inside I do believe that whipping was the final straw on what was inevitable. As a result, I had allowed my life to be held hostage for many years before gaining knowledge of my being a prisoner in a *"Dysfunctional"* situation. *"Dysfunction is a word that has been used to describe family breakdown in ways that has proved to be damaging to its future growth!* That's a frequently used word in society and really deserves to have a permanent place at dinner tables, in schools, in the news, movies and anywhere else people speak about family matters. It totally fits my family as a whole growing up and you may feel it applies to your circumstances. Unfortunately, our country has become overwhelmingly dysfunctional for various reasons and it is somewhat the norm in the minds of most. There are clearly too many cases where people have allowed anger to dictate how they respond to adversity. It is obvious that much of our country's problems stem from fatherless situations, even though many will contest to absentee mothers becoming a growing problem. We surely need to discuss mothers in another setting. My goal is to assist you in moving beyond blame in your life and bring you to a point of overcoming such issues. Surely the undesirables exist, but it shouldn't hinder you from having a peaceful and productive life. Like mine, I hope your unpleasant memories can someday be used to help others get up, dust themselves off and move toward better days.

"Dysfunction is a word that describes family breakdown in ways that has proven to be damaging to its future growth!"

Do you sometime find yourself wondering why you were dealt a hand in life which snatched a very important person from you? This is a similarly common thought when it comes to us wanting a father who was present to nurture, be a role model and provide security. Reactions such as hurt, anger and blame are expected, but you should avoid allowing them to fester long. Whether or not someone was present to express how special you are does not dictate your level of importance. You must develop a mindset that you are Gods VIP and to stop wasting time or energy on being disappointed. This will require an attitude of complete determination, because hurt is hard to overlook. Just know that you are in an extremely large group of people with similar situations and often hearing first-hand accounts can help your personal issues. There is probably 80-90% of this country in your category and many have blamed themselves for the negative actions of another person. This is simply a distraction from opportunity and hope.

[10] *For we are God's masterpiece. He has created us anew in Christ Jesus, so we can do the good things he planned for us long ago. Ephesians 2:10 NLT*

Another great lesson I've learned was to never allow lack of attention from my parents to hinder my personal responsibility and progress. Life has been full of ups and downs where people close to me have let me down, but I am no longer beating myself up for their inappropriate

---

attitudes. This is not just a fatherless problem; however, I tend to believe it is more common and promotes negative behavior than other issues. The _Greg's rule_ has been to *"take every bad experience and turn them into a positive"* or simply put, *"turn lemons into lemonade".* This seems to be a better way to handle situations I can't control.

Have you ever considered that his father could have failed to demonstrate character or was simply not available? In my case, I never met my grandfather on my father's side. In most cases, we never take a moment to think on how less of a father our fathers had. Maybe he never had a foundation of responsibility poured into his young mind, creating his behavior. I didn't mention that to discount their lack of responsibility or to be insensitive of a medical problem or death. More importantly, my purpose is to open minds to realize we all must begin to stop the revolving door which takes us nowhere fast. Most of us don't know many of our relatives from past generations well enough to know or address potential reasons. Older family members at times won't share what matters to avoid embarrassment and I feel we cannot allow that to stop forward progress. My way of thinking about my family has taken me to a point of *"What once was does not have to be what will be".*

Final Point:

"In order to place blame, we must first know and understand our father's past in order to cure the bitter symptoms."

We must be honest with ourselves in order to release blames of any kind. This may include the negative actions of others against us. Please take a moment and address the question below:

CHAPTER SUMMARY:

EXERCISE:

1. Write down guilty or blame matters you experienced against yourself or others.

    - _____

    - _____

    - _____

    - _____

2. Mark the one(s) you place blame on for your fatherless situation:

    _____Your Father

    _____Your Mother

    _____Yourself

    _____Others _____

3. Briefly explain what you feel would take to remove blame off yourself or others.

    _____

    _____

    _____

4. Find two or three people you are close to whose parents are divorced (**_NOTE:_** _List no names, document as Subject #1, 2 & 3)._, and ask them two questions:

1) Do you feel you were part of your parents' marital problem?

   1st Subject: _____   2nd Subject: _____   3rdSubject: _____

2) Has your life been negatively affected after the divorce? If yes, in which way? Briefly describe their responses:

- SUBJECT #1:

   _____

   _____

   _____

   _____

- SUBJECT #2:

   _____

   _____

   _____

   _____

- SUBJECT #3:

   _____

   _____

_____

_____

NOTE: *Asking such questions are not to become nosey, but more importantly it will show you how others have dealt with a divided family. Your questioning session will probably spark up an interesting/rewarding conversation. There is no need to divulge your responses in this book, because you are going through a refining process.*

ABUSED

When dad whipped me with a thin steel rod as a little boy my mind recorded that moment as a lifelong traumatic nightmare. Dad reacted in a way that was not like him, but as a child I felt I was experiencing physical abuse. It only arises now when various situations occur in my presence (*i.e. when I witness or hear of children being verbally or physically abused*). For a brief moment, my mind flashes back as a child and causes me to mentally retreat back under my bed for protection from potential harm. I can generally tell when children or adults have been traumatized in some way and my prayer is it will not haunt them for a lifetime. The truth is my feelings were hurt more than that object, because I'm now certain he wasn't trying to physically harm me. This event took over thirty years to overcome and still today I tend to relive the moment when and after those licks were delivered. This book primarily focuses on fathers, but the truth is much of my abuse didn't come from my father.

When we explore the various actions above, there will always be the question of *"Why me?"* These two words have haunted millions of adults throughout their life and have followed a majority to their graves. That helped me realize society need to address several questions and begin healing from such emotional and damaging experiences.

Most of us have pretended during some point of our lives and that is what we are going to do at this moment! *"Imagine being born where your father's lack of presence was never an issue and most of all expressed love toward you. Think of the decreased anger you might display and the increased desire to love on others around you. Even greater than that, think in terms of how fewer crimes would have been committed".*

Alright, now shake yourself out of the dream and return back to reality! From a realistic perspective, it didn't smell like a bed of roses for most of us. Instead it stunk! Didn't it? The reason it seems to be a hint of anger in those words, is because it's truly present! Certainly, this doesn't mean that I am using that force of anger in a negative way. Just the opposite is true. I have learned to turn my *"Why me?"* pity party into *"Why not celebrations?"* and you should do the same. The *"Why not?"* allows you to become active in removing destructive strongholds, which in turn will hinder future growth.

Abuse can come in various shapes, sizes and manners and you should understand your status before moving onward:

1. There is **Verbal abuse** which allows words of discouragement, to degrade and cut you down like a double-edged sword, building emotional scares. It is difficult to become the great person you were created to be when a self-centered/controlling parent decides to call you dumb, stupid, lazy, ignorant, say you will never become anyone special or even treat you in a degrading manner.

2. Then there is **Physical abuse** that makes the victim feel helpless and in some instances, cause some people to feel that form of behavior is normal, when it is not.

There's one very sensitive area many people refuse to address, because of the shame it presents. Sexual abuse towards children and teenagers at the hands of family members, baby sitters, school administrators or other students are the most trouble areas. These acts against our children leave me to believe a large number of these situations could be prevented, if fathers were more involved or available to help protect them. Many mothers are not able or simply too irresponsible to provide such protection. Absences of fathers leave room for the perpetrator to think they have a green light to violate. We are constantly hearing adults mention how their lives changed after such physical attacks. Adult victims have trouble with relationships and trusting others. One can only imagine, what long lasting negative experiences a person endures during a lifetime. My children always were told what I would do to someone who harms them and in their minds a protector was available. For those who do not have a caring or available father around trouble lurks like an animal waiting on its prey. Even good caring mothers cannot do it all!

3. Lastly, we are plagued with **_Psychological abuse_** and it can be a very destructive form of abuse to get out of your system.

   *Psychological abuse, also referred to as **emotional abuse** or **mental abuse**, is a form of abuse characterized by a person subjecting or exposing another to behavior that may result in psychological trauma, including anxiety, chronic depression, or post-traumatic stress disorder. Such abuse is often associated with situations of power imbalance, such as abusive relationships, bullying, and abuse in the workplace. [Source: Wikipedia]*

To sum it up, it is very clear that *Verbal and Physical abuse* are a part or bi-products of *Psychological Abuse*. Unfortunately, our homes, workplaces, churches, the streets and prisons are filled with people who *are/were* exposed to an abuse which caused them to lash out at others. You often hear that after the admission of a hideous crime a person will blame their childhood abuse for their behavior. *What if this book can help reduce the cycle of ignorance towards others?* I want to say, it can and will by starting with those of us who have been victims of inappropriate or unfortunate situations.

Of course, there are many others we could have listed, but the point is there's nothing that can erase the harm experienced. I wanted to get you stirred up before attempting to cut the hurt away from around your heart. You might want to call me a heart surgeon at this point, because my goal is to leave you with a brand-new heart. Your new heart will allow opportunity for positive change that will not only benefit you; more importantly, your own children and others around you will reap harvest.

Lack of a caring father and abuse or loss by death has led to people giving up on life when they had so much to live for. Sad to say, some abusers are no longer alive and the hurt still exists! The abuser cannot and will not steal who you want to become and I pray you will believe greatness is on the way soon!

"10 The thief's purpose is to steal and kill and destroy. My purpose is to give them a rich and satisfying life." John 10:10 NLT

Final Point:

"While we are wasting energy and time remembering painful moments and lost opportunities, blessings are passing us by, so don't be bogged down with tricks of the enemy's tricks."

Dr. Fatherhood

CHAPTER SUMMARY:

EXERCISE:

1. If you or someone you know has been verbally abused, what unpleasant words did you experience or hear (*i.e. useless, dumb, never amount to anything, etc.*)?

   - _____

   - _____

   - _____

   - _____

   - _____

2. Mark the one(s) you feel fits your personal situation:

   _____ Verbal Abuse

   _____ Physical Abuse

   _____ Psychological Abuse

   _____ Others _____

3. Explain briefly areas of your life that has been negatively affected by selections in number 2:

_____

_____

_____

_____

4. In general, do you believe a missing father sometimes causes an abandoned mother to become aggressive against the children? Explain why?

_____

_____

_____

_____

MIRROR IMAGE

Throughout the course of our life people will mention how we might laugh, sound, look or even act like our father. This is common, even when he has never been present. It was sometimes hurtful and for some reason hearing such comments were taken as a negative when people compared me to my father. I wasn't very proud of the man who never taught me much about life. This is probably true for many of you reading this book, but I have some good news. No, I didn't save any money on my car insurance. However, I've gotten beyond the hurtful feelings associated with being compared to a man who allowed alcohol to dominate his world. Once I determined for myself how different we are as people, no comment of association could affect me again. Hopefully, after you have completed this part there will be closure in this particular area which haunts many people for a lifetime. This does not have to happen to you and your desired happiness.

Most people in society have branded fathers, who seem to not get the task of being a good parent right as being *deadbeats*. I am certain the offenders do not desire being called such names, since it has become a great way to identify men who have proven to be useless to society. Of course, there are always two sides to any story and I would suspect those men who don't have it all together have stories of their own. In order for anyone to understand why fathers are not performing we must first know their negative past experiences. In this part, we will explore just a few areas that fathers acquire earlier in life and carry it like luggage.

There is something I would like to call the **Lack of Attention Plague (LAP)**. The LAP is something many people tend to acquire after living with a parent whose middle name should be "*Who Cares*". Often when this happens the child grows into adulthood and becomes who they despised.

My success in life is contributed primarily to those men who came into my life and shared wisdom and knowledge to help me build character. You must surround yourself with those types of people even if it means walking away from male family members or so-called friends. This is certainly *for the ladies as well*, because we tend to approve of what we disagree with. You might just get someone like your dad, who is in need of prayer and maturity.

EXERCISE: *Close your eyes for a moment.* Imagine having a father around to take you to sporting events or attending one of your own. Remember, to do this correctly, you must imagine him with all of the best intentions and behavior. That imagination is what is needed to look beyond the LAP moments.

Have you noticed something about you as an individual that tend to remind you of your father (looks or habits)?

REFLECTIONS OF RIGHT OR WRONG

I never knew my father's father (*my grandfather*), but after watching my own father it became obvious there was likely a connection between their behaviors. I can imagine my grandfather was not playing the game of responsibility from a father's standpoint. This is not meant to bash our grandfather, but that is something I have asked myself over and over. There is a need to know that information, if it is available.

Have you ever met your father's father? _____

If so, did they seem to be alike in some ways? _____

Explain the similarities:

_____

_____

In today's society, we hear people ask "*Who's Ya Daddy?*" and quite often it has been the brunt of jokes to many people. We choose to laugh at the joke to avoid crying out for help in resolving critical issues from within our hearts. To those of us who haven't experienced having that great father and role model such a statement is more sinister than funny. <u>A good father will nurture</u> his children into the direction of <u>success</u> that will take them to a <u>higher level</u> than themselves. More than often we are not experiencing that type of needed concern for children in homes today.

If someone were to ask me who my father was I would probably pause for a brief moment and say "*I really didn't know the man*". That type of response could potentially be one that many people would deliver, if asked such a question. The funny thing about that is I really don't care any longer. Lingering on that has caused me to lose valuable time thinking about someone who truly did very little for me as a child. This may seem to be a harsh way of putting it, but honestly that is what helped me overcome not having him there for me during moments when I needed his presence.

There is one thing said to many young men who have missing fathers; "*You are just like your daddy!*" This is weird, because some are possibly demonstrating similar behavior characteristics, but I personally don't like to hear that being spoken into their young minds. "*I am myself and no one can be compared to the greatness I possess.*" This is what every person should say and think about themselves. You are who you say you are not what your mama, aunt, uncle or even your grandparents have negatively spoken over you as a child or adult.

Many fathers who choose not to be available struggle with various weaknesses which contribute to failed responsibilities. Here are just a few warning signs of a person who has very little concern about others around them and may have been passed down:

1. *Alcohol & Illegal Drug Usage* – Many call this a disease or habit, but children need a sober minded male role model. People choose to drink or use drugs and children <u>do not</u> choose to be born. For many years, I'd think back on my father's drinking habit and became fighting mad. They are both used to hide an underlining problem that will only

remain suppressed and won't go away. And for a child it becomes a matter of complete rejection. One particular question which still remains in my mind is: *What gave him the right to waste away those precious years of my young life by satisfying his own desires?*

2. *Anger problems* – I have heard people say that *"hurting people hurt people"* and from what I can tell from my personal experiences that is one of the truest statements that I have ever heard spoken. Anger is like a deadly virus that should require quarantine procedures to get it under total control. In most cases the entire family is exposed to a person who probably needs to be institutionalized in order to acquire knowledge of the negative impact. Now, it is very much insane to think many people will change without major intervention.

3. *Never keeps his word* – There is little concern about speaking the truth and not caring about the consequences of such behavior. Very little respect is present when it comes to the children. Dishonesty is a sure show stopper and should never be taken lightly.

4. *Lack of knowledge* – Maybe their father didn't teach them the requirements needed to fulfill their duties as a man, husband or father and they are not comfortable operating in a blind manner. It is almost like getting a new piece of electronic equipment that has a great deal of cool features and not having a manual to show you how it works. The operator would be so miserably lost that they would just take the unit back to the store or just

push it to the side until they urgently need to figure it out. Most often many fathers who leave will need to go back to those they left for assistance at some point of their aging life. *How backward is that concept?*

5. <u>*Lack of Character*</u> – What is character? Webster defines character as: "*One of the attributes or features that make up and distinguish the individual.*" Some live life from day to day and don't even know who or what they are for themselves let alone the thought of someone else. In short; there are a lot of undetermined men who are just running in circles like a dog chasing his tail.

6. <u>*Just plain self-centered*</u> – I figure for those who don't fall into either category above will probably meet this particular one. It's very true to say selfish actions harm a child's future when they don't receive attention in their younger years.

When we decide to try and do what is right, there is a strong chance our level of maturity will take hold and keep us from giving in to such weaknesses. Knowing our father's potential trouble spots may just help us help them correct and improve. Keep in mind, not every man realizes how to harness the ingredients associated with being an active father when they didn't have one around.

BREAKING THE CYCLE

Some behavior can be generations deep, but the great thing is you can be the one who will wipe the slate clean and create positive family growth. In most cases, we concentrate so heavily on what has harmed us that our minds do not let us see we are actually at the starting line waiting to head for greatness. Just think of how your own children or grandchildren will thank you for stomping out ignorance from the family line. I've forgiven every man in my family who failed to take on their responsibility. You might ask why I decided to do such a thing and my answer would be personal yet simple. The buck must stop somewhere and in order for me to truly progress, putting their mess behind had to take place first. Of course, I still think on those very issues which bothered me for years.

Many years ago, I heard the saying that *"you are what you eat"* and in the same way I truly believe that what you say about yourself determines your self-esteem level. My personal decision has been to never allow anyone's actions, words or feelings dictate who I am and how great I am. You are as great as you say you are!

"24 Kind words are like honey – sweet to the soul and healthy for the body."

Proverbs 16:24 (NLT)

Before we go any further I would like to ask that you have an open mind about what will take place next.

Question: *If your father was like you are today would you be happy?*

If the answer is *no* there is a major problem requiring your immediate attention. For most of us the case would be that our fathers were not responsible individuals and neither are we. As a child watching my father drink his life away gave me the feeling that alcohol was not something I would be consuming, but I was wrong. Years after my parents were divorced I had my first drink as a middle school student. This first drink caused me to gain a habit of my own that lasted over twenty years. Of course, my alcoholism didn't cause my own marriage to dissolve, but there were major problems created from my habit. I am certain my children looked at me in the same way that I looked at my own father. It became obvious to me when they got old enough to make certain comments about my drinking habits. After realizing and admitting I had taken some of the same stupid pills my father had taken my attitude began to change. Oddly enough they were some of the same ones I despised from his behavior as a child. Can you believe that?

Do you ever find yourself wondering why you have chosen to repeat some of the same bad habits your father or mother had?

Another classic example is when a man becomes unfaithful to a spouse or in a relationship. This is just one more of the many things people dislike about their parents, but still become a mirror image. Men are greatly under represented when we turn on the television. Society seems to maintain giving men the K-9 name (dogs) or that we are all alike because of the idiotic behavior of many. Unfortunately, many men are only acting out what they learned during childhood and we must avoid following the blind into the ditch of failure.

With that said, you may break the mirror by changing from the negative habits or activity your father might have managed to live out. Even if you haven't met the man or spent much time around him there are probably areas of your life that could use change for the better. Just think, if you were unhappy watching your own father live an irresponsible life, your own children will think the same or worst about your actions if they see him in you. Many people have mentioned that they didn't know their father, but are operating in a manner that dictates a need for change. Whether he was around or not we all acquire bad habits that need to be addressed.

We must ask ourselves these three thought provoking questions:

- *What will our children remember about us?*

- *How much of our life have we shared with our children?*

- *How much of their life have we allowed them to share with us?*

Below write, every action by your father that you consider being /have been bad habits and then indicate whether or not you are presently repeating those very acts. Even those things that you may be afraid to share with others should be at least observed and strongly assessed in your mind. Remember, admitting that you are repeating acts that are embarrassing is a start toward correction. Don't be afraid to clean out your little closet, because it will become a walk-in filled with many great things for others to emulate.

LIST YOUR FATHER'S BAD HABIT(S):

Things I Dis-liked about
my father:

Am I repeating this habit/trait?
(circle one)
Explain Why?

1. _____   YES or NO _____

2. _____   YES or NO _____

3. _____   YES or NO _____

4. _____   YES or NO _____

5. _____   YES or NO _____

LIST YOUR FATHER'S GOOD HABIT(S):

Things I liked about my father
or someone shared with me:

Am I repeating this habit/trait?
(circle one)
Explain Why?

1. _____   YES or NO _____

2. _____   YES or NO _____

3. _____   YES or NO _____

4. _____   YES or NO _____

5. _____   YES or NO _____

BORROWED SURVIVAL SKILLS

There is much lost when a man chooses not to be a vital part of raising a child up to be a successful adult. At times we must gain wisdom and knowledge from men outside of our childhood homes. This may even happen when a father is there doing his best, but quite often as we reach adulthood there is still much to be learned. When no man is around for whatever reason to share what a young man or lady needs to face the world a sense of urgency follows. Many times, when a void exists the lessons come from undesirable people who need help themselves (i.e. music, movies, sports figures, etc.).

How far are you willing to go when it comes to gaining the very elements only a father can truly teach or provide you? I can truly say that my personal journey has reached places like Illinois, Germany, Kentucky, Turkey and the entire book of Proverbs in the bible. Wisdom, Knowledge and Understanding are key essentials to help us move from one level to the next and my childhood moments didn't offer much of either.

While discussing this subject, it is very easy to think about Role Models and the impact they have on our lives. A role model is generally spoken of as one individual, but I want to introduce something new. My personal definition of a role model includes many people that I have encountered over the years. Sadly, to say, I give no one person other than Jesus that title, because what has made me who I am today includes more people than I can count on both hands. Best to my memory, I would like to illustrate what I call my *Circle of Role Models*. This consists of a representation of society who stepped in directly or indirectly to mold me into the man I am today.

GREG'S CIRCLE OF ROLE MODELS:

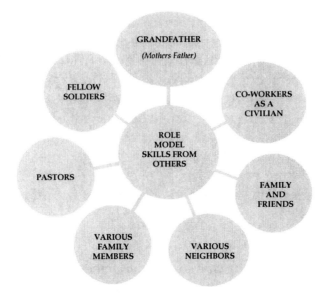

As you can see, there are many people included in my circle of Role Model status. I totally commend all of the people who believed in my skills, abilities and potential over the years as I slowly grew into the man I am today. While discussing this very concept with a friend I realized there are cases where a person with a great father may still have role models outside of that father. This is by no means a negative toward fathers who do what's right. It just shows how many of us require a little extra to become the great men and women life offers. Sure, people I do not personally know have molded me in some way, so I can easily say they are in my circle. We all have a number of people positively affecting our growth process.

Never allow sports, television series, reality shows or movies to create your role model base, because you are almost guaranteed to become disappointed. We become who we believe in and I have always been a person who limits that area of focus. That is my main reason for saying Jesus earlier. The bible has never disappointed me in my journey to grow as a man and I am not ashamed to say so!

YOUR CIRCLE OF ROLE MODELS:

Take a few minutes to place those who might have given you something potentially missed by the father not in your life. If you have more than allowed spaces feel free to add more circles. Remember, the more the better, in a world where knowledge is powerful. You will find these to be helpful later in the book as we proceed to a higher level of understanding.

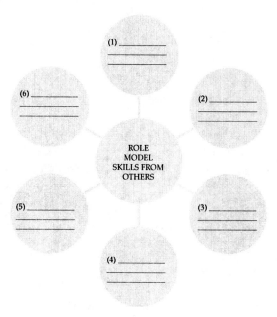

REFLECTIONS: *Explain how each one listed has influenced your life in a positive way (List by number and feel free to expand on additional paper):*

_____

_____

_____

_____

_____

_____

_____

_____

_____

_____

My own personal experience of not having a father to teach me the ropes of how to be a man, husband or father may seem to be a mystery as wisdom flowed from my conversations. Even as a child I knew something important was lacking from my father. Much worst, I sensed getting more from him would be out of the question. This observation angered me for many years and while in my early twenties I decided to forgive the lack of effort on his part and focus on my own children. The question still lingered in my mind as to who would give me what was required to gain wisdom and become successful. One particular day an idea swooped down hitting me like an anvil. In a roundabout way, I asked this question: *Why not borrow wisdom and knowledge from everyone you come in contact with and avoid holding on to aggravations of not having a father to show or teach you?*

From that point on I began to grab onto anything someone had to share that provided knowledge or wisdom. If it has something to do with faith, fatherhood, trustworthiness, finances or life in general my ears, mind and heart were wide open to receive. There have been hundreds of people (young and old) who have contributed in making me who I am today. I often joke about having many fathers. That means I am a man with many mentors of different/ various backgrounds. The majority of them have no idea what they have done to and for my life.

EXERCISE:

- Take your mind off of all other concerns.

- Imagine that the man who chose not to be responsible in your life never existed for a few moments.

- Now set back and think of all of the times you had a conversation with another man who cared enough to share a life changing thought or wisdom with you.

- Write down every beneficial bit of advice you can remember provided by those other people who were not family or friends (use additional paper, if necessary).

_____

_____

_____

_____

_____

_____

_____

_____

- Shut your eyes for a moment and think to yourself about all of the many faces your father can now have. (**<u>NOTE:</u>** We have not brought your natural father back into the picture yet).

Once you have allowed yourself to go through this brief exercise, breathe easily. Everyone realizes fathers are supposed to provide love, wisdom, knowledge, support and much more. In the real world, many times that is not the case. However, knowing those things can also come from others is a breath of fresh air. Never allow yourself to be limited by the lack your own father gave you. Better yet, take advantage like I did by gaining knowledge and wisdom from anyone willing to share.

STEPFATHERS

The role of a stepfather is frequently treated as if they are not important, leaving many of them very little hope of getting the credit they deserve. Think for a moment about a man who has chosen to raise someone else's children as their own and unfortunately are disrespected. Many of them are told by the children *"You are not my daddy and can't tell me what to do!"*. Most have stepped up to the plate in an attempt to be and do their best, but are frequently faced with obstacles. Of course, there are many stepfathers who tend to be like the man who abandoned the children. Drinking, drugs or abuse may even become an added, unpleasant feature.

Have you found yourself wondering why children reject love given by stepfathers who try very hard to replace an absent father? I can't understand why most kids will create an undesirable relationship with their stepfather as though they hate or want to get rid of the man. Many men who marry a woman with children by another man more than likely want to be accepted by the children. There is a high percentage chance that he would like to make a positive difference while raising them. It is very uncomfortable for a man to be treated in a bad way when he is trying to make things work with rebellious children he didn't bring into this world.

I don't recall telling my own stepfather *"You're not my daddy!"*, but there have been large numbers of men who have been pushed away with such comments. This statement generally is coming from a child who is trying to cope with not having their biological father present. Let's be realistic, if your real father isn't man enough to take on his responsibilities maybe you should at least give the other guy a chance. Of course, that is if he is not a man with bad habits that does not foster healthy surroundings. What do you have to lose? With that being said, I am not trying to discount the pain associated with a missing father. I wanted to bring this up because of the growing number of people who finally meet someone, want a fresh start and must have the support of their children. Certainly, there are many guys who are bad stepfathers, and must be addressed in accordance to their motives.

You are special and special things are supposed to happen to your life. Unless your stepfather fell or falls into the category of other ill-behaved fathers, I would suggest you honor them. I have had two and even in their worst moments I've respected them. They never personally caused me harm from an abusive standpoint and I thanked them for that with honoring them as my mother's husbands. They were/are not the type of motivators or mentors I would have liked around me as a child, but I made the best out of what was given to me. These guys deserve that much from a child who can't remember much about his own father. The best part of my story is I have been extremely blessed by my respect of authority at any level. Not saying I wanted to waiver because of their wrong choices, but even into my adulthood they received respect.

QUESTIONS:

Did you have a stepfather? _____

How was your relationship with him? _____

_____

_____

Was your relationship rocky at first and got better with time?

_____

_____

If applicable, do bad feelings still exist?

_____

_____

THE FLIP SIDE

By now you have either gotten angry, sad, confused or became enlightened from the previous sections. My intent, as mentioned earlier was and is to help you overcome the absence of your father; no matter how the separation took place. As we have focused primarily on our fathers it is fitting to also examine ourselves. Before pressing onward, I would like to assess you as a potential or active parent. We have a responsibility to become better parents than those who raised us, whether they were good or bad.

ASSIGN A RATING FROM 1 – 10 (*w/10 being best*):

Where do you rate your mother? _____

Where do you rate your father? _____

If you are a parent, where do you rate yourself? _____

If you are not yet a parent and would like to be one someday, where would you rate yourself based on your current maturity level? _____

REMEMBER: *If your parent or parents were 5's you should strive to get closer to the 10. This approach will ensure generations to follow will only improve from our unpleasant past experiences.*

The purpose of this segment is to open your mind, heart and actions up into new phases. Whether you are a parent, would like to become one or for whatever reason will never have the opportunity, there is a responsibility to know how to perform as one. There is always a need or opportunity for us to mentor, nurture or just motivate others to become better. This is always true unless you live in a world where you are the only human on earth.

<u>**NOTE:**</u> *Just think, your children may not put a high number on you, so always be conscious of your performance as a parent.*

One warm day while at a gas station I overheard a man yelling and cursing at a child who was around six years old or younger. Fussing or correcting is alright, but the words of profanity towards the child were filling the air like a rapid firing weapon. My first thought was to approach him in an attempt to rescue the poor kid from the garbage being dished out at him. Of course, my brain over wrote my heart and I did nothing to keep from getting into an altercation. His behavior indicated to me that he had no concern about being a good influence, neither did he exercise self-control. The very opposite is what was demonstrated. This led me to believe him to have been treated in the same manner as a child. To put a child through the behavior directed at us as children is wrong and must be addressed immediately.

"⁴ Fathers, do not provoke your children to anger by the way you treat them. Rather, bring them up with the discipline and instruction that comes from the Lord."
Ephesians 6:4 (NLT)

As you strive to overcome the hurt or loss of your own father, it is very important to build character as a great parent yourself. This book could have easily included mothers, because of the destruction many of them have caused us. Instead, my immediate concern is on the devastation caused by men on families and society.

I've also observed young children up to teenagers talking to their parents like their peers. In those cases, I either make comments in a way they'd received correction or simply watched in disbelief. My concern in each situation is that we as parents are allowing bad behavior to follow our children into adulthood. Often, we are allowing this type of activity to make up for some void in the family unit. These bad behaviors could be the result of a fatherless home, fear of what the child may do, a parent wanting to give freedom to express, etc., but each one carries heavy risks. I am certain many of the young men I've spoken to in prison or jails can attest to one of these being in their past.

There is a great chance that most of the children in these categories are living without a responsible father or have one who has no love or care about their futures. See where you fit in.

QUESTIONS:

Are you a parent? _____

If not, would you like to be one someday? _____

Does it bother you when a child is disrespectful to a parent or should they have a right to express themselves? Please explain your position in this matter.

_____

_____

_____

_____

SESSION III:

MOVING FORWARD

- Moving Forward
- Fresh Start
- Esteem Yourself
- Putting the Past Behind
- Hope

MOVING FORWARD

I hope the first two sections rattled your thoughts and emotions in a way where you want to heal from the mess forced into your life as a child. No matter how your father was vacant from your life, the damage can be remotely identical. This is not to say there aren't many unfamiliar roads traveled in each ordeal, but the destination of loss ultimately will be the same. As I had mentioned earlier, my hope is you will have taken a moment to read reason outside of your personal experience. By doing so you were able to somewhat get into the world of those who actually experienced these particular cast of events.

While thinking about my approach to help you move forward an analogy came to mind; *"We have been given gifts at birth, various situations can stagnate growth. Take the **seed**, **tree** and the **fruit** for example. If the conditions are not correct the <u>seed</u> may never become a tree and the tree will not produce fruit! In many cases people are much like that, but our advantage is there are avenues for us to gain important life nutrients of wisdom, knowledge and understanding to gain a fresh start. In other words, our roots may be dry, but our fruit can't die."*

It has been said that <u>good things</u> <u>cannot</u> be rushed. Now, prepare yourself to start experiencing the very elements which will take you to greater heights than you can imagine. If you haven't in the past, get ready to live in a world of being or experiencing:

- *Happy – Being able to enjoy having peace and laughter even when unpleasant memories overshadow your daily activities.*

- *Hopeful* – *Know with certainty that your future will be better than your past.*

- *Humorous* – *Understand how important it is to find things to laugh at no matter how your things look.*

- *Joy* – *Finding pleasure and happiness in things.*

- *Love* – *Realize how loving you first will create a better environment for you, your family and others around you.*

- *Security* – *The feeling of being safe.*

- *Sensitivity* – *Help break the anger cloud that cause people to treat others and situations in a very aggressive manner.*

- *Stability* – *Being stable in your life and as you deal with life's difficult situations.*

- *Strong* – *Being confident about the ability you already have inside of you to overcome any situation that will follow after this book.*

Just think back and remember who this book was written for (*i.e. Young Men, Men, Young Ladies and Women*) and notice how every plague and situation could have affected each category. Now you must simply make a determination to incorporate what was missing from your childhood into your own parenting responsibilities and break the chain of pain. Your action today will benefit generations in your family and others around you will catch on to what is right.

Below is a chart that will help open your eyes in a way to hopefully bring out issues that have negatively affected you. Quite often we focus directly on our own family situations and never realize how others around us contribute to our issues. Please follow the guidelines of completion below and I will explain further following this exercise.

WHICH OF THESE VIRUSES PLAGUED YOUR LIFE OR AFFECTED THE LIFE OF OTHERS YOU KNOW? (<u>NOTE</u>: *Don't allow suppressed feelings and emotions to hinder your selections or comments.*)

<u>GUIDELINES OF CHART COMPLETION</u>

#1 = *"Fatherless Viruses"* discussed earlier.

#2 = Mark *the Viruses which have affected you* with an (X).

#3 = Enter a number between 0 and 3 indicating *"Level of Impact on You"* (see responses below):

> 0 = <u>No</u> further concern
> > 1 = <u>Less</u> noticeable
> > > 2 = <u>Often</u> an issue shows up
> > > > 3 = <u>Major</u> problems still present

#4 = Thinking of helping *family members, friends* or others with their own copy of this book?

#5 = Include a *comment* to reflect on at a later date to see when things improve.

NOTE: *As you saw earlier, there are more than one on my list, to included #4, because my helping others have assisted in my own overcoming efforts.*

#1	#2	#3	#4	#5
FATHERLESS VIRUSES	WHICH VIRUS AFFECTED YOU	LEVEL OF IMPACT ON YOU NOW	HELPING A FAMILY MEMBER, FRIEND OR MORE	COMMENTS
Abandoned before birth, at birth or during childhood				
Father Passing Away during your childhood				
Incarcerated for an extended period				
Illegal Drugs or Alcohol				
Divorce of your parents				
Medical Condition interfered with relationship				
Absentee Father (i.e. *They're in the house, but not involved.*)				
Your Father's Father was not there for him				
Military Separation causing family breakdown				

After addressing these comparisons, we can begin the process to assist you in moving forward into better days. As your life improves, there are greater chances for you to help others who might have experienced any fatherless viruses. My helping others cope has been a valuable asset in my overcoming process. Many times, we feel our situations must be perfect before assisting others and that is far from the truth.

No matter how many viruses you've chosen, the amount does not dictate your level of need for overcoming. You could have selected one and have a huge amount of baggage associated with that particular plague. Like an addiction, we are in control of the future and the past will continue to have the same storyline.

FRESH START

In order to consider moving forward we must determine what is required to help us heal from the years of painful experiences. There is a great need to make a fresh start and press toward a life which delivers happiness. I must be honest with you and mention that my mind occasionally drifts back a tab and anger flares up when my personal experiences return to mind. Steam may flow from my ears and my eyes may even tear up, but that is where it stops. This is normal for anyone who has been through some traumatic events. No one can truly say they forgive and forget all bad things that happened to them. We must however totally forgive in order to press forward. The forgetting area is virtually impossible, unless you have that part of your memory terminated from your brain somehow. Some will tell you to forgive and forget, but if you smack that very person, ten years from now they will recall the moment, pain and humiliation. I am a realist and will remain truthful while helping you overcome.

You may suffer from traumatizing experiences, but you can surely overcome that trauma and move beyond the hurt, pain, mourning and disappointment. At this point, if you have read this entire book your response will not be of one who would say *"yeah right"* in a sarcastic manner. I have been as brutally honest and straight forward as possible in order to pave the way toward fostering greatness out of you.

Please maintain your open-minded status while reading these last chapters in order for positive change to take place in your life. As mentioned earlier, there are situations discussed that have nothing but unpleasantness written all over them and must be addressed as change happens.

Father's Day seems to be a very important day for me in the sense that I have become a father and have been on duty as required. On the other hand, I do think about my own father as my children shower me with gifts, kind words and acts of appreciation. The unfortunate thing I believe about my father is he never was taught how to be a good father, so he failed in that area. We must strive to be examples of change for the young men and women coming up, if the minority is to become the majority. Even though I appreciate Father's Day, there is a part of me that dreads the day. I mentioned this concern to show I have issues in this area even as I write this book. My strength has been to identify issues which negatively affect me and my life while gradually improving. Some have taken years while others are much quicker to cross off my *overcoming list*.

ESTEEM YOURSELF

Are you one of those people who have gone through life constantly waiting for someone to pat you on the back? Many of us have this particular problem of wanting others to boost our ego in order for that good-feeling rush to appear. Maybe you depend on esteem from a spouse, family member, friend, co-worker or even that mean boss. That is a very dangerous precedence, because quite often no one will be there to provide such an injection when needed the most. By the time you have finished reading this chapter I hope you are patting your own back and esteeming yourself. Of course, the previous statement doesn't mean to discount the praises of others; it strictly means you should avoid waiting for the outside encouragement when it may never arrive.

You might be wondering why I am including this subject in a book about overcoming a father who didn't care. If asked to explain my reasoning I would probably respond with a question. Why do people end up reaching out to others for self-esteem shots? There are several answers that come to my mind:

1. Do you even know how you really are?
2. What level of value and trust do you place in yourself?
3. Were you always put down by your father or others?

Stop doubting how great you are just because your father didn't instill encouragement inside of your young mind. Remember that your self-esteem level can be as high as you want it to be without input from outsiders. I know because mine stays at an 11 on a scale of 1-10. I know that may sound silly, but there is a great deal of truth in that statement. I refuse to accept being de-motivated in a world of predominately self-centered people expecting them to pat me on the back. I must be at a high level of self-esteem in order to help others, so there isn't time for me to wait on what may never take place. Stop fearing failure and begin speaking words of success into your own heart on a daily basis. Life can be a drag when we depend on outside influences to make us feel or think better about ourselves. Of course, be careful to avoid becoming arrogant or self-worshipping. That could prove to be a big problem with relationships. There is a balance and nothing is wrong with others giving you encouraging words, because we all need and like the attention.

How do you feel about yourself as a person (i.e. mother, father, brother, sister, friend, etc.)?

_____

_____

_____

Do you wait on others to give you compliments before believing yourself? Why?

_____

_____

_____

_____

"Each day must begin with you speaking, thinking or feeling great thoughts about yourself. Trust me, no one else will do so on a continuous basis! A missing in action or the loss of a father should not create a negative overtone throughout your entire life."

Greg Campbell (Dr. Fatherhood)

PUTTING THE PAST BEHIND

- Capture the avenues to release errors that affect your life
- Forgiving both alive and deceased fathers who don't/didn't care
- Letter of forgiveness
- Dialogue
- How to release past rejection, hurt and pain

"Suffering from a fatherless wound can lead to a significant amount of trauma and peril for anyone. However, there are several contributing factors that can influence a father's absence from their children. The fact remains the same the child that is fatherless suffers a significant void. One way to overcome the hurt of being fatherless is through forgiveness. Forgiveness is the first and sometimes the most tangible element in overcoming the absence of a father."

MR. EARL WASHINGTON, MSW, LCSW
Director of Children Services

A sense of anger lingered for some time within my heart after my father passed away in 1995. Of course, I had expressed love toward him for many years before losing him, but the verbal forgiveness never took place. Months had passed when I realized my hard-felt feelings deep down from not speaking to him about my dissatisfaction. He was very ill for many years and had changed his life in such a traumatic fashion that correction was not an option.

Losing a father during the years when you need them most can be emotionally disturbing during those innocent childhood times. Whether you are too young to understand what has happened or old enough to mourn the effect somehow it turns out to be the same. While growing up it's easy to notice the other kids getting attention from the father that still remains and you often wonder, "What if?". Of course, in the back of your mind, the painful words of "Why me?" will keep you focused on what hurts.

After encountering the abundance of issues surrounding the absence of a father who didn't care enough to nurture you as a child you must make a move. Most people I have talked with in my lifetime will say that they can forgive people who have hurt them, but they won't forget the action. Nearly every one of them had a look of <u>un-forgiveness</u> plastered across their foreheads. Some were bold enough to verbally express their feelings and assured me of what they would do to the man if he came around them. Many that I have kept in contact with are experiencing low levels of success and I am certain it is directly connected to not forgiving others.

Below I have prepared a sample letter for those of you who are blessed to still have a living father to share this forgiveness process with. Unfortunately, my father never was able to receive a written letter, but I made sure my heart and communication with him never expressed anger toward him. Let's just say my life has been much greater than he probably had ever dreamed for his own. Yes, this greatness came when I forgave his self-centered behavior that negatively affected me and the rest of our family.

For many people, their father passed away before an opportunity to gain a needed relationship occurred. Maybe he never was there to provide the vital nurturing a child requires to become a productive adult. Deep inside or even closer to the surface you just can't understand why he would have treated you in such a manner and the anger grows worse. This is a normal reaction to display after anyone has wronged you when they were supposed to love and provide for you. Aggravations of this kind **do not** have to continue haunting or disturbing your every wakening moments like a chronic decease. The choice of removing undesirable feelings like these can only be one you exercise.

Letter of forgiveness or closure to your father: (sample only)

I'd recommend you prepare a letter to your father similar to the one below. Remember, there is a need to _write a letter regardless of whether he is dead or alive._ Writing a letter to a father who is deceased, showed very little interest or never showed up may bring needed closure. The letter is for the other person to read, but most important it is for you to cleanse your heart from pain or hatred. Below is a sample only and I do recommend you write your letter from the heart and as long as you desire.

GREG'S UNDELIVERABLE LETTER TO HIS DECEASED FATHER:
(He passed away in 1995 and it was not too late to write a letter of closure!)

....

"One morning I woke from a dream that was so real that compelled me to write this letter below and once you read it, I hope you will understand why."
Dr. Fatherhood

Dear Dad,

You passed away many years ago, but I still have those moments when seeing fathers with their children make me wonder, what if? All I can think of is how great it would be to have experienced a hug or hearing the words "I Love You". No memories created has left me with nothing to cherish or remember! However, my lack of your presence as a child caused me to focus on being a caring husband and father regardless to what did or didn't happen.

I still love you and forgive your behavior which allowed drinking to medically take you away from being the father I really needed as a young man.

Sincerely,

Your Son,
Greg

"Overcoming often requires us to make personal changes while preparing to move forward! It is not always about the actions or lack of actions by our parents or anyone else!"
Dr. Fatherhood

"[13] Make allowance for each other's faults, and forgive anyone who offends you. Remember, the Lord forgave you, so you must forgive others."
Colossians 3:13 (NLT)

SAMPLE TO ASSIT YOU IN GETTING STARTED:

Dear Dad,

I am writing this letter to inform you that your lack of participation in my life as a child caused me great personal problems. It has come to the point in time where I must officially forgive your actions or the lack of action and begin to grow. The best way to completely achieve this goal is to totally release you as the guilty party for my not having a father to nurture me in my younger years. Maybe there are some personal reasons or habits which caused you to not be around.

This letter is not meant to alienate you out of my life, but it is meant to show that I can do great with or without your presence. My ultimate desire is to have you in my life, but that choice will strictly be left up to you to accomplish.

In spite of all that I have endured I want to let you know that I love and forgive you.

Sincerely,

Your (*Son* or *Daughter*)
YOUR NAME HERE

•••

Now if you know where he is located and feel up to sending it to him, please do so. On the other hand, for fathers who are no longer living, writing the letter is just as important. You may choose to take it to the cemetery and read it <u>*without distractive bystanders*</u> who may not care or understand. This process is strictly for your growth.

At this point, I would imagine you are getting a little angry at this one-sided approach by yourself. Trust me! This is a normal reaction to such a task until you can totally understand the benefits from such action. I once heard a song mention how *life is like a game without an option of replay*. This thought must be taken to heart when attempting to put the unpleasant events in the past to rest. Just remember, you can't turn back the hands of time, but you sure can control your future successes and happiness. Just that thought alone was enough to turn my heart toward greatness.

Whether you are young or old the negative past must be purged from your mind and heart. Start focusing on your own actions and how you will build a positive legacy of you own.

We have addressed a few critical elements necessary to help overcome your missing father. By now you probably realize that your father didn't demonstrate affection because he was treated in that manner. Therefore, you no longer need to be haunted with the question of self-worth. The past can become a foundation for hope or become a vice for destruction. My negative experiences were rough, but as long as I can think like an overcomer, they tend to matter less and less.

Now it is time for a brand-new start, so your children will make a list of great things they will be proud to share. Greatness is in you and nothing anyone else has said or committed against you will be the defining factor of your successful future. Join the ranks of survivors who refused to give up and settle for less from not having a father involved. The best of your life starts right now so sit back and enjoy the fruits of fulfillment.

"13 No, dear brothers and sisters, I have not achieved it, but I focus on this one thing: Forgetting the past and looking forward to what lies ahead,"

Philippians 3:13 (NLT)

HOPE

Over the years, I have learned to ensure my wellbeing is intact, so when assisting others my level of confidence reflects. This always help others become comfortable in allowing a once broken young man to help them up from their mess.

As we discussed earlier there were others outside of your father who might have instilled wisdom and knowledge into your life. We called them the *Circle of Role Models* from me as the author and you as the reader. In this portion take a moment and reflect on those you have imparted life application skills into over the years. In order to make you feel better, find someone else to do something for and your own situations will surely improve! This is important to address, no matter what age you are. There are two questions to address:

In order to make you feel better, find someone else to do something for and your own situations will surely improve!

THE QUESTIONS ARE:

1) *Whose circles do you feel you're in (i.e. family, friends, etc.)?*
2) *Whose circles would you like to be in at some point (i.e. family, friends, etc.)?*

WRITE DOWN BELOW: *WHOSE CIRCLE YOU MAY PERSONALLY BE IN?*

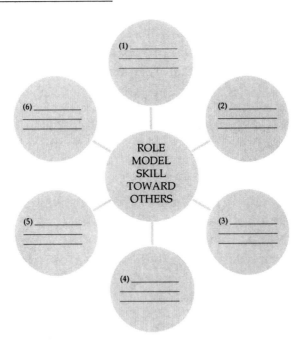

If you have filled in any of the entries, there is a probability these individuals did not have their father around either. Just remember; when we touch the growth process of one person, generations benefit in a great way. Part of your overcoming must include your reaching out to help others do the same.

••

NOW WRITE DOWN BELOW: *WHOSE CIRCLE YOU FEEL YOU SHOULD BE IN? (Insert the names of those you want to impact in a great way, so they may include you in their circle chart someday).*

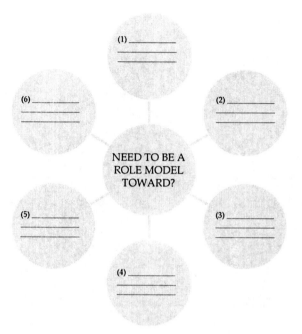

(1) _____

(6) _____

NEED TO BE A
ROLE MODEL
TOWARD?

(2) _____

(5) _____

(3) _____

(4) _____

As we prepare to conclude our journey of overcoming a missing father I would like to personally commend you for taking the time to recall your past while feeding your future. Helping us improve will always come easier when we take time to help others through difficult times. That is what I have attempted to do for myself in writing this book.

SO MUCH IN COMMON

As we discussed the various reasons for fathers who have become MIA there is one thing not yet mentioned; that is the fact, many if not all, have *a great deal in common*. Of course, we tend to look at them as separate actions or situations, but there is much more to gain when we realize the similar outcomes or impact brought on by their very existence. After discussions with many people affected by each virus or plague mentioned, my conclusion was those impacted shared strikingly close stories. Yes, the pain and much discussed were different, but the loss from the absence was somewhat the same. Below I have provided the discussed viruses and many overall impacts:

FATHERLESS VIRUSES	BIRTHDAYS	SPORTS	LOVE	ILLNESSES	NURTURING
Abandoned	X	X	X	X	X
Father Deceased during your childhood	X	X	X	X	X
Incarcerated for an extended period	X	X	X	X	X
Illegal Drugs or Alcohol	X	X	X	X	X
Divorce of your parents	X	X	X	X	X
Medical Condition interfered with relationship	X	X	X	X	X
Absentee Father (i.e. they're in the house, but not involved)	X	X	X	X	X
Your Father's Father (Maybe, not there for him)	X	X	X	X	X
Military Separation	X	X	X	X	X

Now you know, you're not alone in your journey. There are millions of people feeling your pain and much worse. The reason I included this portion was to allow you to begin a healthy dialogue with others. Now you may begin not only making your surroundings better, but just maybe there are others requiring your gained insight.

It simply does not matter why we didn't have our fathers, but the outcome has always been the same.

The hurt, pain, and loss remain essentially identical in most cases. I would hope you were able to gather the important facts laid out in order to begin overcoming and moving forward. This country is depended on us to get it right in raising our own children with love and respect. We must begin repairing the root of society's problems that lead to bad relationships, abused children becoming abusers, and causing people to feel poverty is normal.

Your determination to complete this book will surely create a new way of dealing with what has been discussed. Hence, I would like to say to:

1. **YOUNG MAN**, you now know that being *a real man* requires *maturity* and *responsibility* and nothing good comes from negative influences. Strive to gain wisdom and understanding of ways to try not to let your children become victims of fatherless causes, at all cost. *No matter how young you are as a father the responsibility is yours when it comes to doing what is right. That means, your parents or grandparents should not be doing those things you are naturally supposed to be doing. Think on terms as to how you want to be treated as a child and it will make being a father much easier!*

2. **YOUNG LADIES**, remember that you are special no matter how the past or present may want to dictate to your heart. You deserve a future with a husband and father of your children that loves you for who you are. Real men will work hard to provide for their children without pressure

from you or the court system. Some men are good looking and that is where their value stop, so don't be hoodwinked by vanity and find yourself all alone with his child or children. When a man rides your financial coat tail, the children will suffer with you and their future will be negatively impacted. Never allow yourself to become a victim of circumstances you have control of. It takes two to <u>work </u>for financial success. *Know that <u>you are beautiful</u> inside and out and never allow your <u>self-esteem</u> to be dictated by others!*

3. <u>MEN,</u> you have the greatest responsibility to do what is right and be the real man and father. After speaking with hundreds of men who were impacted by one or more of the viruses, something very obvious stood out to me. Their stories strongly suggested, there is a great need for men to become leaders and positive role models. Allowing personal past experiences or what others think of you can hinder progress. Many of us have taken the wrong roads of life and caused our children to wonder *"what in the world"* is his problem. Like an alcoholic or drug addict, the first requirement to improving is admitting you have a problem. With men, the major hindrances are pride or ego and I too have suffered from those road blocks. Real men work on ways to become better communicators and strive to not repeat bad experiences from their fatherless situation. To do this we must have other men we trust to discuss this with, without them resorting to providing bad advice. Men who speak in such manners are more than likely harboring their own tragic

passed father matters. *Become a man of integrity and honor, so your children or younger family member will have quality to look up to!*

4. **WOMEN** (*single or married*), knowing the important factors surrounding the impact of a fatherless environment can now help you determine why you make various decisions. If your relationships have been questionable in the past, you may now begin building a foundation of hope. Understanding how having a father involved during your earlier years can greatly improve your approach to life in general. Gained understanding also enhances your ability to parent or help others in situations where there isn't a father there for the children. Never create an environment where your children's father can't assist in nurturing their growth, unless a court deems him incompetent. Your failed relationship should never be the reason for your children to be distanced from their father. They will surely question why at the right age. Many times, over compensating in the absence of a father can lead to extreme emotional drain and illnesses, but now that burden can end and a new you can begin! *Know that you are beautiful inside and out and never allow your self-esteem to be dictated by others!*

5. **FATHERS,** who seem to have experienced the void of a male role model can now avoid falling into the same mold as their fathers. My children call asking for advice and I truly believe it is because they trust I care about what matters to

their lives. Wise men are now realizing *it isn't too late to live up to responsibilities with raising or nurturing their children. Recycled hurt and pain only cause repeated behavior that only harm our future generations. Become an agent of change by encouraging other men (young and old) to do the same!*

NOTE FOR ALL: Learn how not to dish out lemons like the many people who have channeled anger and disappointment incorrectly. Our homes, streets and prisons are filled with hurting and angry people who need what you have read. We no longer have time to make excuses when we can begin shaping a better future! There is much more to my story and if using excuses had been my route I could have become a hard-core criminal of some sort. Instead, I chose to let that *rear-view mirror experiences* just push me forward. Thanks for taking this overcoming ride and I hope you will someday share your story in a way to help others move out of despair.

EXERCISE:

NOW LET'S TURN LEMONS INTO LEMONADE

This exercise is being revisited to allow you to see how far you have grown and what areas needing more attention. Believe me, reading this book will not cause immediate change for everyone. There are going to be many who will require referring back to the book from time to time. That requirement is perfectly alright and does not indicate a weakness or lack of hope on your part.

PRESENT FEELINGS & ISSUES

1. Mark your present feelings or issues in #2 _without_ referring back to your previous chart at the end of _"Who Should Read"_ regarding your fatherless situation.

2. Once you have completed this task flip back to the initial chart and compare responses. You may proceed with transferring the previous results at this point.

	#1 Date:	#2 Date:	#3 Date:	
WHAT APPLY TO YOU?	INITIAL RESPONSES	WHICH APPLY NOW?	6 MONTHS LATER _(Revisit)_	REASON FOR RESPONSE CHANGE, IF ANY? _(i.e. this book, recent event, etc.)_
Abandoned				
Abused				
Abusive				
Anger				
Depressed				
Forgotten				
Frustration				
Guilt				
Hateful				
Hopelessness				
Hurt				
Ignored				
Low self-esteem				
Rejected				
Resentment				
Sad				

Safety				
Shame				
Shy				
Tormented				
Unloved				
Unsociable				
Unstable Relationships				
Violence				
Worthlessness				
HOW MANY?				

(NOTE: You may once again place additional feelings or issues on a separate piece of paper, if necessary.)

To determine how well you have progressed there is a blank 6-month follow-up column on the above chart. Please mark your calendar on your wall, computer or cell phone, so you may revisit and gauge your new status. Stages of success are critical to establish how well you are overcoming!

1. Your initial feelings naturally may never completely change, but the way you deal with your surroundings and situations will ultimately become more manageable.

2. Once you begin to overcome what seemed impossible you will see why I chose to write this book and share parts of my experiences.

Congratulations, you have invested in your family's future growth towards greater days and remember to not repeat or use the negative actions of others as excuses to settle for mediocracy!

Dr. Fatherhood

SPECIAL THANKS TO:

My wife, children, grandchildren, son-in-law's, extended family and friends who have always encouraged me along my journey. Love and blessing to them all!

Editors: Kirtrina Marie Quisenberry (*my daughter*) , Jacquelyn DeVeaux, CSW (*family friend*) & Marion Peeler, MS Counseling & Education (27 years)

PHOTOGRAPHY: Richard Lockette of *"2 Locks Production"*

BARBER: Pat Bryant (*Lil Pat*) of 52 Platinum Cutz"

Most importantly, I would like to thank God for helping me become the man I am today and for placing people in my life to replace what I missed from my own fatherless moments!

CPSIA information can be obtained
at www.ICGtesting.com
Printed in the USA
FFOW02n0109280318
46080675-47047FF